Your Dream Catcher

DREAMS
COME
TRUE

How to Live the Life of Your Dreams

by

David Kline Lovett

Your Dream Catcher

Also by David Kline Lovett

Books

101 Reasons to Love Your Real Estate Agent
Comedy Made Easy
The Right Real Estate Agent Can Make You Rich
also available as Ebooks

Coming soon:
365 Tips, Tricks, & Techniques for Public Speaking

Native American Flute
CDs and MP3s

Dream Catcher
Enchantments
Meditation Music

Life-Transformative
CDs and MP3s

Be an Outstanding Student
Close More Escrows
Closing the Sale
Confident Speaker
Get a Girlfriend
Jump Start Your Network Marketing Business
Landing Your Dream Job
Pathways to Weight Loss

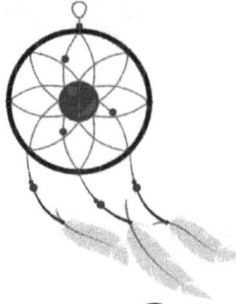

Your DREAM CATCHER

How to Live the Life of Your Dreams

Copyright © 2018, David Kline Lovett
www.davidklinelovett.com
godimhappy@me.com

Your Dream Catcher
Self-publishing

ISBN 978-0-9971362-2-7

Special Thanks

to

Rev. Dr. Joanne Coleman

Acknowledgments

I'm grateful, first of all, for life. For whatever or whomever made this wonderful world and gave us the ability to live, to love, and to laugh. I'm so blessed to be alive at this time in history in this wonderful country, and have the ability and freedom to write this book, to share joy, happiness, and bliss with the world.

I am thankful to my coach, friend, minister, guru, teacher, and comic genius, Dr. Rev. Joanne Coleman. This book would not be possible without her encouragement and pit-bull-ish-ness. (I know that's not a word...yet). Rev. Joanne gave me the tools, the confidence, and the knowledge that I'm good enough. Thank you.

I acknowledge Rev. Kristina Collins, Rev. Karen Rice, Michael Bernard Beckwith, Jim Baker, Marian Camson, Jessie James, and David White Cloud Burkheart, who have all nurtured, taught, inspired, and encouraged me to believe in myself. You have all inspired gifts and talents. Thank you!

Special thank you to Furaha Golden who took my personal photographs, Shelly Greenhalgh-Davis, my amazing editor, Rekhaa Gopinath for the incredible front and back cover designs.

Contents

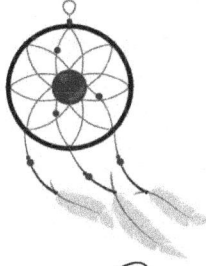

Your
DREAM CATCHER

Introduction

"If you can DREAM it, you can DO it."

~Walt Disney

Could there be something missing in your life? A feeling that there is a void, an emptiness? Do you spend much of your time, efforts, and energy literally running in a frantic attempt to fill the void? Do you tend to stay busy in an exhausting effort to distract yourself? Are you consuming your life with work, school, working out, reading, pets, watching television, sports, church, alcohol, or drugs?

My friend Gail goes to church on Sunday morning and the Wednesday night service. She takes classes on Tuesday, Thursday, and Friday. Granted, this is an amazing church with plenty to offer. Five times a week, no matter how wonderful, is a little much. Not because celebrating God and learning about praying, meditating, and Jesus are in any way negative. It's obvious that Gail is avoiding something. Gail is running at such a frantic pace there isn't any time for her to examine her own life. She knows about the life of Jesus, but regarding the life of Gail, she's a little fuzzy.

"You can't realize your dreams unless you have one to begin with."
~Thomas Edison

Gail is afraid to examine her life. You have read the Socrates quote, "The unexamined life is not worth living." For Gail, the examined life is just way too scary. What if she found out she isn't perfect? What if she discovered that she makes mistakes, errors, and blunders? What if she uncovered the fact she fails…often. Gail unconsciously tries to do everything and anything to avoid examination or reflection, and in so doing, she can't truly live. She can't truly dream.

Your Dream Catcher will allow you to safely examine your life, to dare, choose, and chart your dreams. You will learn the value of not only having a coach, but more importantly, to be coachable. You will be left with an ability to recognize and transform your inner saboteur, to love your body so you can have the ability to live the life of your dreams. Be inspired, motivated, and invigorated to move toward your dreams. You will learn to succeed and to take care of your dreams on a daily basis. You will find a method to identify and follow your intuition. You will see the benefits in treasuring your family and living your kindest life while you vow to your dreams.

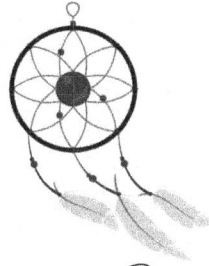

Your
DREAM CATCHER

Chapter I. Dare to Dream

"Somewhere over the rainbow, skies are blue, and the dreams that you dare to dream really do come true."

~Harold Arlen

Author of The Wizard of Oz

Your dreams may be buried deep inside, put aside, or even forgotten. Your dreams are a key to having the life you want. Why not dream your wildest, biggest dreams? If Don Quixote could dream the impossible dream, so can YOU! Dare to dream your most far-reaching, seemingly most unattainable dream! You have a calling, a goal, a wish, or desire you have put aside, thinking that someday maybe you might get around to it. This is the place, and now is the time to dare to dream.

It's time, right now, to START. I dare you to dream. It all starts with a wish, a desire, a longing for something more, bigger, different, new, and exciting. What are your hidden and wildest dreams? It doesn't matter that you have put them aside, thrown them away, or even forgotten them. It's time to bring them back. It's time to believe you can live the life of your dreams and have the life you want. It's time to *Dare to Dream*!

Kids dare each other to do crazy things all the time. They dare each other to do things that they want to do, yet are too shy or afraid to start. When we want to try something but are afraid, we often get someone else to try it first. Getting others involved in your dreams is a method that will also work with you!

There are dreams you want to make real but may have to be pushed, nudged, and maybe shoved to get started. You can simply dare yourself to do it. Get a coach, friend, or family member to support you and your dreams. Now, you are not alone when you take that step, jump, or leap.

I love the movie *Back to the Future*. Marty McFly, played by Michael J. Fox, is dared by the town bully Biff Tannen when Biff says, "McFly, are you a chicken?" Biff dares him to a fight but is twice the size of Marty. The dare (being called a chicken) motivated Marty to take on Biff despite the size difference and his slim chance of success.

You can dare yourself to dream your own impossible dream. In reality, you know that there is no dream that is impossible. Be unreasonable in your dreaming. What would you dream if you couldn't fail? Dream those things you never thought you could, should, or dare to dream. Call yourself a chicken. Have your coach, friend, or relative ask you to be unreasonable in your dreaming. Dare to dream that impossible dream. I double dare you!

Dreams

* a series of thoughts, images, or emotions occurring during sleep
* a strongly desired goal or purpose
* something that fully satisfies a wish

Merriam-Webster

Catch your dreams

Dreams Never Die

You do need someone to dare you, to call you a chicken, because dreams never die. Your dreams stay with you, within you, no matter what. You can live your dreams, or you can let them sit dormant. Your dreams sit like a smoldering fire ready to be reignited. All you need to do is take that first step toward your dreams. You don't often have a school bully around to motivate you. You need something like this book as a guide to help you to catch your dreams.

You don't really have an alternative. To fully live, you must live your purpose, passion, or dreams. Your alternative is to sheepishly sit on the sideline and never get into the game. Sitting on the bench is a choice, but what is the use of living a life on the sideline? As Reverend Rick Warren wrote in his book, *A Purpose Driven Life,* "If you have felt hopeless, hold on! Wonderful changes are going to happen in your life as you begin to live it on purpose." A life of purpose, or living the life of your dreams, is built into your DNA. When you are not moving toward your dreams, you are fighting against nature. Without dreams you don't really have a life. When you are simply and only making a living, that's not living. Your dreams will always be in you. Your dreams may simply need a spark to be awakened because your dreams never die.

Uncover Your Buried Dreams

Dare yourself to rekindle your dreams, especially the big ones. Step up and confront your hesitations. Use your own inner Biff to motivate yourself. It's imperative to your really living, to getting on the court of your life. It is imperative for you to uncover your buried dreams.

Brainstorm and note your wildest dreams with a friend. Carry a notepad or use a smart phone and make a note when you think of something you desire out of life. Go to sleep with the intent to wake up remembering some of your childhood dreams. Take out a pad and pencil and free write on a blank sheet of paper whatever comes into your head. You can start ferreting by writing the word 'dream', and keep writing the word 'dream' until something more comes. What do you love? What would you do if you didn't get paid for it? What would you do if you didn't have a care in the world? What would you do for free? Who would you do it with? Where would you go?

Make a list of your successes. When you were in school, or as a child, what were you good at? What sports or activities did you like the most? Everyone has something special to offer. You have your own gifts to give, your unique offerings to share with the world. This is why it's so important to dare to dream. You can't in good conscience withhold your gifts and talents from the world. The world deserves to share in and experience your dreams. By not daring to dream, you are deeming your light and not living the life you were born to live.

When I heard Robert H. Schuller say, "What would you do if you couldn't fail?" I was mesmerized by the thought. What would you dream if you couldn't fail? What would you aspire to if there was no chance of failure? What would you write, sing, make, draw, build, create? What buried dreams could be uncovered just by believing you couldn't fail?

What is your passion? What is your deepest burning desire? Take a moment and let it come to you. If there was no one to laugh at you, to criticize, put down, or ridicule you, if you had no fear, what would you dream? If magically you knew there could be no failure, what would you dare to dream?

> "Every great dream begins with a dreamer. Always remember, you have within you the strength, the patience, and the passion to reach for the stars to change the world."
> ~ Harriet Tubman

Dream Fearlessly

Let go of your fear of success, failure, not looking good, or looking bad. Let go of that inner fear that repeatedly screams, "I'm not good enough." Let go of that fear inside that is so strong that you forget about your dreams. Let go of that fear that drives, dominates, and determines your day. Let go of that fear that if left unchecked, will stifle your dreams for days, weeks, months, years, and even a lifetime.

You most likely learned as a child to worry about how others perceived you. You may have been obsessed with how others thought, analyzed, and judged you. You could have been worried about your appearance, fitting in, and being accepted at any cost. I dare you to dream as if none of that existed.

You need a dream that is bigger than your fears. Your transformation begins with a dare. You were born to accomplish your most unreasonable, amazing dreams. What is it that motivates you? We all have that button that can stop us or inspire us. What is the button that will get you started on your dreams? Do you have to be called a chicken? Do you need a coach to hold you accountable? Do you have to be backed up against a wall?

I simply dare you to dream. After all, why else are you here? What is your purpose in life? If it is not to live your dreams, what is it? Do you want your headstone to read, "Here lies someone who could have lived their dreams, BUT DIDN'T?"

Do you want to waste your life as a couch potato? Is the idea of wasting years, decades, maybe your entire life doing things you aren't passionate about sound good to you? Do I have to call you a chicken? Do you need a coach? Do you need to visit a graveyard? Whatever is your button, push it. I dare you.

Dreams Your Gateway to Greatness

It is good to know that working toward your dream will also bring greatness, satisfaction, and contentment. Wake up to the fact that moving toward greatness will require some discomfort on your part. We often feel discomfort when we are engaged in a new activity. A strategy to get you moving toward living your dream is to find and move past your growth edge. Your growth edge is the place where you feel uncomfortable. Most often this is where you are confronted with something new that you haven't done before. The idea is to go to your growth edge and then step past it. Try something you haven't done before; for example, enroll in a dance, photography, or acting class you have been hesitant to take.

You can find your edge by clarifying and expanding your dreams. If your edge is allowing yourself to dream, that is your growth edge. The trick is to push just past where you are comfortable into an uncomfortable place. Spend time daily in that uncomfortable place until it's no longer uncomfortable, and then step a little farther out until you feel uncomfortable again. You will feel excited and a little scared. Constantly pushing past your growth edge will be a major factor in you living your dreams.

Dreams truly are your gateway to greatness. Your dream might be to be a great friend, daughter, or son. Being a great son, daughter, or friend is a wonderful dream to achieve. Now, I dare you to dream another.

You may know the story of Jim Carrey, the actor and comedian. Jim had a dream to be a famous and wealthy movie star. Carrey wrote himself a $10 million dollar check, postdated it a number of years in the future, and put it in his wallet. Almost to the day of that postdated check, Jim Carrey signed a contract to make the movie *Mask* for, you guessed it, $10 million.

Dr. Martin Luther King, Jr. had a dream of equal rights, Dr. King's dream continues to manifest today. The light of Dr. King's dream has never gone out. Just like the light of your dreams, no matter how faint, has never gone out. Your job is to fan and fuel that fire, and as Winston Churchill said, "Never, never, never give up." Live the life of your dreams that you were born to live. Catch your dreams.

Be your own dream catcher. You don't have to be a movie or television star, or lead a civil rights movement to achieve your dreams.

Playing it safe is living a life that is not worthy of who you are. Know that your dreams are a gateway to greatness. Your dreams and passions will guide you to success, contentment, and fulfillment. There's something magical about having a dream, a magic that will make your dream a reality.

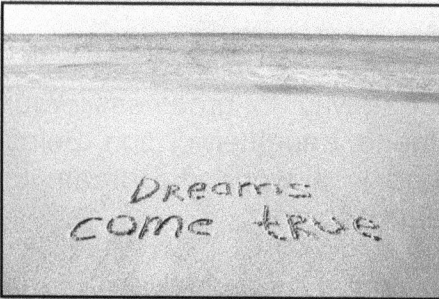

DARE

* to challenge to perform an action especially as a proof of courage
* to confront boldly
* to have the courage to contend against, venture, or try

Merriam-Webster

Dreams Are Your Guides

Your dreams will be your guide. When you listen, synchronicity happens in regards to your dream; the magic will magically occur. You will meet the right people, discover the right information, and the perfect opportunities will present themselves to you. The synchronicity created by your dreams will become your guide.

Would a ship captain just get on the boat and go? A ship captan has a plan. He or she would know where the boat is, its destination, and the exact course needed to get there. Your dreams, goals, and plans will direct you to the people, places, and things you will need to make it to your destination. There is a magic to having a dream that will help you. Your passion and desire for your dream will serve as fuel for your journey.

Your passion for your dreams helps to clarify what to do, where you may want to do it, and when is the best time to do it. Working toward and for your dreams will move you toward and past your edge. When engaged in moving toward your dreams, moving past your edge can be a pleasure rather than any kind of pain. Fall in love with your dreams. The book, *A Course in Miracles,* says in effect, "You don't have to understand what to do next. Just do it." In other words, take that first step.

Take your dreams with you wherever you go. Sleep with your dreams. Don't let them be a secret. Put them on the wall, the refrigerator, make a dream board, write them on a sheet of paper and put it in your wallet, or purse like Jim Carrey did. Keep your dreams in your mind. Think about them all the time; notice the synchronicity going on in regards to your dream; keep a journal so you can document the evidence. If you aren't aware and paying attention, you won't notice the synchronicity and guides with which they gift you.

Play with Your Dreams

Have fun with your dreams. Having fun with your dreams is paramount to your living them. Life can be very serious; dreams should be easy and fun. Play with them. Life is meant to be enjoyed. Dreams are about singing, dancing, laughing, and creating. Enjoy your dreams, and enjoy the road you travel toward your dreams.

Dreams are much better than a goal. Dreams are from your deepest, most creative self. Dreams are flexible and changeable and respond to your creativity. Dreams allow your creative side to play. This flexibly allows your dreams to go where they want to go. Not how we have predetermined how our dreams should go. Dreams allow us to adjust and flow according to our individual creativity.

"This is no time for ease and comfort. It is time to dare and endure."
~Winston Churchill

You are Your Dreams

In reality you are your dreams. Your dreams define who you are. Without dreams, you are a ship without a rudder. You are not fully utilizing your gifts and talents. Your dreams determine your actions. Sharing, striving for, and achieving your dreams are a wonderful contribution to the world. We have no idea on how much our striving and working toward our dreams influences, inspires, and motivates others.

When you are in the midst of living your dreams, you are paying your gifts forward. Whatever you are doing, wherever you are, people will see and sense something special in your step. They will see it in your face and in your upbeat mannerisms. I know when I move into my growth edge when moving toward my dream, I feel better about myself. Feeling good is a signal you are on the right track. No one ever accomplished anything great by not taking a risk or by giving up. You feel better, and that rubs off on everyone else. Dream large. Live your dreams fearlessly. Jim Carrey didn't write a million dollar check; he wrote a $10 million check! Dr. Martin Luther King's dream of civil rights wasn't just for the people at his church; it was for everyone.

Dream Notes

To Jump-Start Your Dreams
Ask yourself-
What If…
What if…
What if…
&
Why Not?

Never Give Up

Dream big and never give up on them. In some respects, you are your dreams. Your dreams give you purpose and a reason to get up in the morning. Giving up on your dreams and purpose would be to give up on life. We all have setbacks, distractions, and/or discouragements. I dare you to dream your biggest, wildest, most fantastic dreams. What is your alternative? No one truly wants to live a life without dreams or purpose. You want more out of life. You want to have a reason to get up in the morning. You want to make a difference in the world. By not giving up on your dreams, you are not giving up on yourself.

It is how we react and respond to setbacks, distractions, and discouragements that determines whether we live our dreams or not. You must not give up. In 1940, all of mainland Europe had fallen to the Germans. The fate of the people of England seemed hopeless. This is when

Winston Churchill preached, "This is our finest hour." If things seem hopeless, this is your finest hour. So often it is when things seem worse that something wonderful is about to happen. Don't give up. Things will get better. Remember what Churchill repeated, "Never, never, never, never give up."

When things seem the worst; when the setbacks, distractions, or discouragements pile up; when things seem most absolutely desperate, at these times when you want to go buy a gallon of ice cream and turn on the TV, that's when you're at your growth edge. You're right at the threshold of starting to live your dreams. That is when you are most likely to give up. That is why you can never give up. It is always darkest right before the dawn. When things are at their worst, that is when you want to say, "This is good. I'm at my growth edge. I may not feel like it, but today, I'm taking action." It's human to have some setbacks, distractions, and discouragements. Remember, you are worth whatever it takes for you to catch all of your dreams.

If a tiny island country and Winston Churchill can stand up to the Third Reich and the Luftwaffe, you can stand up to whatever is seemingly in your way. When things seem the most difficult is when you are the closest to a breakthrough. England won the battle of Briton with willpower, determination, and grit. You can do so much more than you can imagine, more than you could ever believe, when you dare to dream.

Truth or Dare

Dare to dream and stand up to your fear. Your dreams are your true self, not your fear. By living your dreams you can contribute to the world and have purpose in your life. Accept the dare! The alternatives are to watch television; stay in the same boring job; never take that class, write that book, or dance that dance. It may mean not meeting that special person and not ever going to Paris. We all are going to die eventually. Do you want to say at the end of your life, I played it safe? Or that, "I truly lived my dreams!"

You came into this life for a reason. You want to have purpose and meaning in your life. Your dreams are the key to living that life. Dreams are your gateway to success. Your dreams are your truth. I dare you to live your dreams. To try or not to try, that is my dare. Start by doing the exercises for this chapter. Clarify your dreams. Give your wildest, most passionate dreams life. Allow your passions to rise to the surface. Without a doubt, before you finish this life, you must try. The truth is, all we know for sure is we have this one life. Make the most of it. Dare to dream.

You have no choice, but to dare to dream…

> "Thoughts are but dreams till their effects be tried."
>
> ~William Shakespeare

Conclusion

There is nothing more important than for you to live the life of your dreams. For a variety of reasons, your dreams may have been buried, put aside, and even forgotten. Life, family, work, doing what you thought was more important can simply get in the way. And, what can be more important than living your dreams?

When you dare to dream, when you dream fearlessly, when you stop and realize your dreams are your gateway to greatness, your dreams become real. Allow your dreams to guide you. Play with your dreams, and realize you are your dreams. Most of all, never give up on yourself. Never give up on your dreams; they will never give up on you. You will begin to be your own dream catcher when you dare to dream.

Catch your dreams

Dream Catcher

* a circular framed net with a hole in the center that is used by some American Indian peoples to help block bad dreams and catch good ones

Merriam-Webster

Recap — Dare to Dream

Dreams Never Die: your dreams are always with you.

Uncover Your Buried Dreams: dare to rekindle your fondest dreams.

Dream Fearlessly: let go of your fear of success, failure, and having to look good.

Dreams Your Gateway to Greatness: allow your dreams to move you forward.

Dreams Are Your Guides: your passion for your dreams brings you clarity.

Play With Your Dreams: being playful creates creativity and joy.

You Are Your Dreams: dreams define who you are, so you might as well dream big.

Never Give Up: you are worthy to live your dreams.

Truth or Dare: your dreams are your truth; dare to live them.

Dreamtime
Do Try This at Home

1. What are you passionate about and/or love that you haven't gotten around to doing? Are there childhood dreams you have put aside? Do you have any deep desires you may have buried inside? I dare you to list at least five dreams.

1. _____

2. _____

3. _____

4. _____

5. _____

2. What could you add to make your life more enjoyable, fulfilling, fun, or exciting? Dare to list at least three.

1. _____

2. _____

3. _____

3. What would you do if you couldn't fail and money or time were of no concern? Write as many things as you can, and then write a few more.

_____

_____

_____

_____

_____

_____

_____

_____

4. Free write, (writing whatever comes in mind) for at least five minutes regarding your wildest, most exciting dreams. Are there any repeated messages or themes? Go over all of your dreams, desires, and/or passions from all four exercises. Make a top ten list and then choose the three you want to reach first. These are the dreams you will focus on in this book.

_____

_____

_____

_____

_____

_____

_____

_____

_____

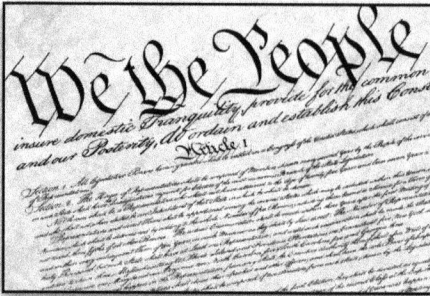

Declaration: Today I dare to take at least one step toward the life of my dreams.

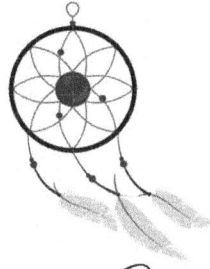

Chapter II. Chart Your Dreams

"Follow the yellow brick road."

~The Munchkins in *The Wizard of Oz*

If you don't know where you are going, how will you know when you get there? If you're moving, growing, and learning, you might as well be moving toward your dreams. The journey is where most of the fun and rewards are anyway. To make the right moves, you are going to need to chart your plan of action.

A chart is a diagram. Your chart can have detailed information or simply be an outline. A chart is a navigational tool to transport you from confusion to self-fulfillment and your dreams. Your chart can be a simple drawing showing the basic shape, layout, and workings of your plan. This chapter is about having a map or guidepost for you to make sure you are headed and constantly moving in the direction of your dreams.

Charts are great because they give you a visual representation of your journey. The exercises at the end of the chapter allow you to chart and design a starting and ending point and a map on how to achieve your dreams. You will be able to see, read, and monitor your progress. You will be able to make course adjustments just like a ship or an airline captain.

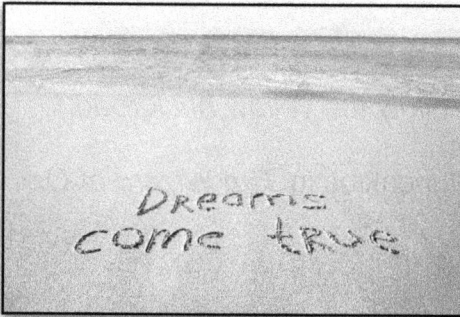

Chart

* a sheet of information in the form of a table, graph, or diagram

* make a map

* a geographical map or plan, especially one used for navigation by sea or air.

Merriam-Webster

Start from Where You Are

A chart is a diagram to map out relationships between two or more variable quantities, as is the relationship between where you are and where you are going. We can all only start from where we are. It's important to be honest and not be ashamed that we aren't closer to our dreams. It's only human to think you are not where you want to be. In truth, we are all exactly where we are intended and should be. We don't have to stay in the same place. The only constant in this world is change. You are perfect, exactly, the way and in the place you are. For instance, one of my dreams is to be an excellent husband. As of this writing, I'm not married, engaged, nor do I have a girlfriend. I'm in the perfect place to be in at this time. This is the perfect place to learn and grow into the type of man who can be a great husband. If I was in a relationship, I wouldn't have the same focus to work toward my dream.

Let's take a couple of my friends, for example. Michelle has a dream to own a McDonald's franchise. Jeremy's desire is to earn his GED (General Educational Diploma), the equivalent of a high school diploma. Describing their dreams and how they charted their dreams will help you chart yours.

Jeremy will need to find out exactly where he is academically. He will need to obtain his prior schools' transcripts. The transcripts will tell him what classes he has already completed toward his dream. As soon as he has all the required classes listed, Jeremy can determine the remaining classes necessary to complete his studies. Jeremy will need to choose a school that offers the classes he needs to take, and with the assistance of a school counselor, together they can easily chart a path for Jeremy to achieve his dream. For example, Jeremy may need to only take two specific classes and pass the GED test.

"Trust the dreams, for in them is the gate to eternity"
~Kahil Gibran

Research the Process

Michelle will need to do some research on how to obtain her McDonald's franchise. The information is available from the McDonald's Corporation. Again, she simply needs to know where she is and what is required to reach her dream of owning a McDonald's franchise.

It doesn't matter how close you are to your dream. What matters is that you start. The first thing you need to do after you know what dream you want to live is to make a chart. To make a chart, you need to know where you are starting from and the necessary steps to reach your dream. A great way to do that is though something called reverse engineering. Webster defines reverse engineering as, "to disassemble and examine or analyze in detail (as a product or device) to discover the concepts involved in manufacture, usually in order to produce something similar." Reverse engineering is the process that Jeremy used. For me, I want to be a magnificent husband. To be a magnificent husband, I need to be married. To be married, I need to get engaged. To get engaged, I need be in a committed relationship. Prior to a committed relationship, I need to be in a relationship. Before being in a relationship, I need to make friends. Prior to making a friend, I need to meet someone. In order to meet someone, I need to get myself into a position to do that.

I also have personal work to do. I need to become the person that I desire. In other words if I want an intelligent, spiritual, healthy, honest, sincere, responsible, well-groomed, loving, and kind woman. I must have all those qualities myself. I need to get to know myself, love, and feel good about myself before I can do that with a woman. I need to find out what a woman wants and needs, and doesn't want or need. It's important for me to learn all the qualities that a woman desires in a husband. I'll want to become familiar with what makes a woman feel happy, loved, respected, and satisfied.

Michelle didn't have a chart or plan, but she did have a dream. She could see the kids enjoying their Happy Meals and her giving out the gifts. Don't be afraid to research for your dream. You can Google, go to the library, buy a book, or seek out an expert. There are books about the history of McDonald's. You can purchase a *Franchising for Dummies* book.

Dream Notes

To Jump-Start Your Dreams

Make a list of every Dream you can think of no-matter how large, how silly or how impossible they may seem.

Information will help Michelle in charting her dream because she will have some knowledge in her mind on how to go about buying a McDonald's franchise. She will have an idea, map, or a chart on how to get from where she is to where she wants to be. She will also learn what is not required. Having a chart will take much of the guesswork out of the process. Owning a franchise will feel possible. She may discover that she can even borrow the money for the down payment, so she can learn the financial aspect of it. She can do the research about all the components necessary, and as Reverend Joanne says, "That will land the dream."

Describe and Design Your Destination

Michelle wants a McDonald's franchise, Jeremy desires his GED, and I'm charting a path to be a magnificent husband.

Our dreams need to be described in detail. A husband isn't just someone who walks down an aisle and says, "I do." What are the behaviors and qualities that go into being a magnificent husband? In the Dreamtime exercises at the end of the chapter, you will list the top ten behaviors it will take to obtain each of your dreams. Pick your top three dreams. You can work on your others later.

Here are my top ten behaviors to become a magnificent husband: Also listed as appendix #8.

1. Always see the Divine in her-**No Matter What.**
2. Constantly consider methods to improve her life.
3. Constantly listen unconditionally and speak honestly.
4. Continually give, share, and think of her.
5. Create and maintain a sparkling home and car.
6. Heal my past with my family and myself, love myself unconditionally.
7. Keep myself impeccably groomed.
8. Love myself unconditionally.
8. Love, honor, and respect all women.
9. Maintain a healthy mind, body, and spirit.
11. Study and learn communication, listening, and relationship skills.

I can start living and embodying these qualities now before I meet my wife-to-be. I can make another list of the qualities of what I want in someone else and what they may desire in me. To start, I must be honest, sincere, respectful, and generous. This is a way of describing my destination in detail. You can do it too. Start by imagining your dream, see it in pictures, hear it in words, feel it in your emotions.

You can chart your dreams in pictures. As Napoleon Bonaparte said, "A picture is worth a thousand words." Pictures will help your imagination and creative insights to visualize how realizing your dream will look. Find pictures of, or draw pictures of how your realized dream will look.

"I still have a vivid memory of my excitement when I first saw a chart of the periodic table of elements. The order in the universe seemed miraculous."
~Joseph Murray

Steps, Procedures, and Behaviors

All successful business have steps, procedures, behaviors, or a plan for the business. The United States of America has a Constitution, which is essentially a plan on how to run the country. A sports team has a game plan. Many of us don't have a clue, let alone a plan. The exercises at the end of this chapter will help you write a chart for your life and dreams. My friend Reverend Joanne Colman says, "You start out in the general and move to the specific." That means you first decide what your dream is, and then determine the steps, behaviors, and habits you need to achieve them. If you want to earn your GED like Jeremy, you will need to define what are the necessary steps, procedures, and behaviors. You will need to determine, for example:

- How much time needs to be devoted to study?
- You may need to upgrade or buy a new computer, tablet, or printer.
- You will need to know what applications are required to be filled out and handed in for processing and when.
- You will research what the costs are and time involved in the classroom.
- What books and materials are required?
- What classes are needed.
- Where do you need to take them and when?

I would suggest you write the steps down on note cards and then arrange them in a chronological order that works best and is most logical for the attainment of your dream. This will give you the steps, procedures, and behaviors necessary to achieve your dream.

To be most successful, it is best to be working on the steps and behaviors as a daily practice. It's imperative that you maintain momentum on achieving your dreams. It's a good idea to plan to work on at least one of the steps daily.

It's imperative to have a written plan and in that plan to include the steps, procedures, and behaviors necessary to achieve your dream. Your plan will insure that you know what to do, in what order, and when.

There is something special when you have something written down that seems to make things happen. Brian Tracy stated, "People with clear, written goals, accomplish far more in a shorter period of time than people without them could ever imagine." Once you make a commitment and determine the steps to get there, all the pieces will seem to magically come together to make your dreams come true.

Don't be afraid to rewrite and adjust your steps to make your plans even better. Often we think that a plan is written in stone and cannot be changed. This is not true nor healthy for your dreams. Your path, like a real road, isn't always a straight line.

A pilot flying from New York to Los Angeles will make hundreds of small adjustments during a planned flight. There are bends and curves that make the ride more interesting. On your path to reach your dreams, anticipate that you will make adjustments, changes, additions, alterations, and subtractions.

Make Time, Place, and Space

The first location to make time, place, and space is in your mind. Many of us are so busy we never stop or slow down. Most are continually running and don't take time to think or contemplate our dreams. We have a fear of failure and/or success. We may feel we don't deserve to live our dreams. For me, I keep running so I don't have to think. It might be that I was afraid that I wasn't good enough, smart enough, or educated enough. I believed if I was to slow down or stop, I might die. The fear of death obviously isn't true. However, for many, it feels real.

The first thing you can do is to slow down. Once you take that bold step and give yourself some time, you will find it actually won't hurt you. You can slow down and contemplate your dreams. You can be like the kid in school who got in trouble for daydreaming. Now you will be in a place where you can begin to chart the steps to realize your dreams.

In second or third grade, I got in trouble for daydreaming. What I was really doing was charting my dreams. Miss Kramer scolded me for not paying attention, when in reality, I was doing the most important thing I could do. I was beginning to chart my dreams. Can you imagine living a life without having any dreams? Without giving yourself some time, place, and space, your dreams won't have a place to develop.

The time you take to daydream with your dreams is the most important time you could ever invest in yourself. It's so easy to believe that your busy time is more valuable because we are, well…busy. Without taking the time to chart your dreams, you won't know what direction to go. You may be productive, but you may be productive going in the wrong direction.

A place means having a location where you can chart your dreams. This could be your bedroom, patio, the beach, any place where you can be alone. I like to get my day started the moment I wake up, so my primary spot is my bed. I'll wake up and sometimes just lie there, or most often will sit up and meditate. I will also take a moment right before going to sleep to visualize and chart how I want the next day to manifest.

Space for me is not a physical space but an attitude in my mind. I create an attitude where I'm available to dream. I'm available to receive and accept any wisdom that may come to me.

> **"I feel we need to remind the world about the Apollo missions and that we can still do impossible things."**
> **~Buzz Aldrin**

Organize

It feels good to have a clean, well-organized space -- a clean desk, a clean room, or freshly washed car. Just as clutter on your desk, in your room or car gets in your way and can annoy you, clutter can get on your mind and get in the way of you charting your dreams. Being organized and charting your dreams, in fact, go together. When my room and my bed are cluttered with books, papers, clothes, and what-have-you, the clutter keeps me from focusing on my dreams. When I'm organized, that is what creates the space where I can consider my dreams.

Have your dreams out where you can see them. Put pictures and written statements of your dreams on the wall, in your car, on the fridge. Organize and prioritize and put in order what activities you will take to step toward your dreams. To achieve your dreams, you must establish where you are, where you want to go, and then do some organized research on how to get there.

When you are organized, you won't have to worry. You won't need to guess about what is the next step. Create a journal where you will have a place to contain your next steps. Writing your steps in a journal will make you more organized, confident, and you will feel better. You will know what you will need to do, what to expect, and in what order. Chart your steps on your calendar so you won't have to think or worry about them, or worry about when the steps need to be completed. Know that having your steps written down and then put on your calendar will have amazing effects on the realization of your dreams.

Create a Mission Statement

Most every successful business and organization has a mission statement. Why not you? In the movie, *The Blues Brothers*, John Belushi and Dan Aykroyd were on a mission from God. This is absolutely true. Your dreams are a mission from God because God wants you to live your biggest, wildest, most exciting, fulfilled life. God wants you to dream and dream big. Why not have a mission statement for your dreams? I have a mission statement in my journal and displayed in my office, bedroom, kitchen, and in my car. This way I won't forget what my mission is.

Here is an example of a mission statement from an organization for public speaking, called *Toastmasters:*

The mission of our Toastmasters' club is to provide a mutually supportive and positive learning environment in which every member has the opportunity to develop communication and leadership skills, which in turn, foster self-confidence and personal growth.

My mission statement for my dream of being a magnificent husband is:

My mission is to openly and honestly communicate, always in all ways. I will be continually interested and supportive in my wife's life. To be on a never-ending mission to transform myself into a better husband. To think of her needs before my own, and to create an environment for her to feel and be appreciated, respected, and loved.

You have the opportunity in the exercises at the end of the chapter to create your own mission statement for your dreams. Don't worry about making it perfect. There is no right or wrong way to write your mission statement. The important thing is that you make one. You can always make adjustments to your statement.

Construct a Dream Board

As Napoleon Bonaparte stated, "A picture is worth a thousand words." A dream board is a board where you can visually see your dreams. It is often made from a board where you can draw or place pictures that represent your dreams (see appendix #12). You can cut out pictures, statements, words, and phrases from magazines, the Internet, and you can draw your own.

Be creative with your dream board. You can include the steps you made to achieve your dreams. You literally have a pirate's treasure map. The treasure is the realization and manifestation of your dreams. Your reward is the treasure of achieving your dreams and having a life that matters. The construction of a treasure map is an important step in the realization of your dreams.

You can glue three-dimensional objects onto your treasure map. You can cut things out of a magazine or draw them yourself. You can use real pictures. Your pictures, words, and statements can be any size, shape, and color you choose. You can make a small map for your journal and a big one for your wall. With a map you can see exactly what the steps are. You can see the journey and the destination and the realization of your dreams. There is something special about having something you can see and touch that tends to make your dreams real. If you don't do anything else this week, start on your treasure map.

Catch your dreams

How to Make a Dream-Board

* Decide the purpose of your dream board.
* Purchase a poster board.
* Collect magazines.
* Choose pictures that match your ideal image of the future

Get a Coach

I will go into more details of coaching in the next chapter. Coaching will save you time, help you be more organized, and will assist in developing the best habits and behaviors for your success. Your coach is most important at charting your dream stage for the realization of your dreams. Your coach will help you in the formation of your map or chart.

She will make sure you are headed in the right direction from the beginning. Having a coach will save you from guessing about what to do, and you will have less stress.

A good coach will make sure you begin with the best-suited guidelines, goals, and direction to fulfill your dreams. My coach helped me by taking the time to determine the qualities in a wife that would be most advantageous to my own values, goals, and dreams. My coach saved me potentially years in my search. My coach helped me outline the qualities that best-suited me that were difficult for me to define. She helped me to uncover my blind spots, to discover what was truly most important to me.

My coach also gave me ideas of where I could go to find the type of woman who fit the list of qualities we had outlined. She insisted for me to find my future wife, I include on my chart a visit to yoga studios and to spiritual and meditation centers. This seems so simple, but it took my coach to bring it to my attention.

Track Your Progress

Keep track of where you are and how you are progressing. Compare where you are to where you would like to be. Make course adjustments, re-evaluate your dreams. Are your dreams the same as they were last time you worked on your chart? Don't be afraid to make adjustments. There is nothing worse than going full speed in the wrong direction.

Tracing your progress allows you to celebrate your progress. In my case, I have recently started meeting women who fit the qualities that best suit me. Making the chart allowed me to realize what qualities I desire in a wife, so I would know when I'm meeting women who are the type who fit those qualities. Now I'm motivated to do more yoga and visit meditation and spiritual centers. My chart tells me the best places to go to meet these women, and by tracing my progress, I know that I'm doing the right things to achieve my dream.

Once Jeremy knows what classes he needs and in what order he needs to take them, he can keep track of each step that he accomplishes. He can make a chart and check off each class that he completes.

Conclusion

A building just like your dream, was first an idea, thought, or a dream that someone dared to dream. That building had to have a set of blueprints or a chart to set the completion of the dream in motion. You are doing the same thing by making a plan or a chart for your dream. This way you are navigating how to reach your dream. Plotting a course from where you are to where you want to be is the most important step you can make. You are making visual representations, thought patterns, and detailed step-by-step actions for you to reach your dreams.

DREAMS
COME
TRUE

Recap — Chart Your Dreams

Start from Where You Are: to get to where you want to go, you need to know exactly where you are now.

Research the Process: research exactly what is necessary to reach your dreams.

Describe and Design your Destination: illustrate the details necessary to reach your dreams.

Steps, Procedures, and Behaviors: create a detailed plan.

Make Time, Place, and Space: slow down and take some time to contemplate your dreams.

Organize: eliminate culture in your mind and your space.

Create a Mission Statement: write out exactly what you intend to create.

Construct a Dream Board: a board with words and pictures illustrating the realization of your dreams.

Get a Coach: a good coach is invaluable to assist you in reaching your dreams.

Track Your Progress: keep track of where you are and how you are progressing.

Dreamtime
Do Try This at Home

1. Construct a dream board (see appendix #12), focusing on your top three dreams. Display it where you can see it <u>every day</u>.

2. Write/Journal daily regarding each of your top three dreams, even if it's just a very small note. (This small action will result in huge strides toward your dream). Write about what you are doing, plan to do, and have completed. Add in your journal where you are having challenges and what you plan to do to solve the challenges. Make sure to write what you are going to do next.

3. Determine ten behaviors that will best insure that you achieve each of your top three dreams (see appendix #7). Post them on the walls in your home, office, kitchen, bathroom, and car. Also post it in your journal.

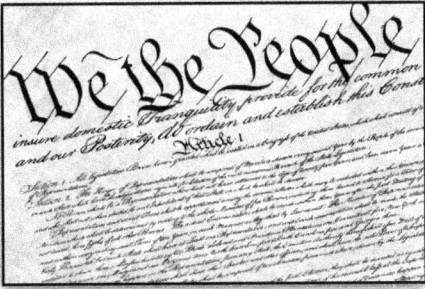

Declaration: Today I lovingly chart my plan of action for the manifestation of my dreams.

Your Dream Catcher

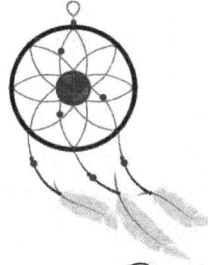

Your
DREAM CATCHER

Chapter III. Become Coachable

"A coach is the best resource to help us achieve our goals and dreams. However, a coach is wasted unless we are coachable."

~David Kline Lovett

In life, we strive to improve, to have, to be, and do more. We endeavor to reach our goals and obtain our dreams. We desire good and avoid what isn't good. The best way to insure we reach our goals and dreams is to have a teacher, mentor, or coach. This chapter takes having a coach one important step further. It would be a dream in itself to have the legendary coach of UCLA basketball, John Wooden, as a personal coach. However, what good would it be to have Coach Wooden as your coach if you aren't ready to learn from him? This chapter will help you benefit and gain the most from the mentor-teacher/student, (coach-coachee) relationship. This chapter will help you help your coach... coach. You will learn how to become more coachable.

Most all of us have had coaches our entire life. Older brothers and sisters, aunts, uncles, relatives, friends, neighbors, parents, teachers, bosses, and our athletic coaches have all been our coaches. I never gave these relationships much thought. I never considered how I could assist my older brother or sister to teach me. I never stopped to think about what I could do to make it easier for my algebra teacher to teach me. Honestly I oftentimes did as little as I could get away with.

You can actively work at increasing your readiness for your coaches, teachers, and mentors. You can start by giving them honest feedback and communication of what you know and where you are unclear. You can come to your classes and meetings early and stay a little after. You can come prepared. You can do some research regarding whatever you are working on. You can do all of your homework plus some extra. Michael Jordan and Kobe Brant would be the first ones at practice and the last ones to leave, sometimes hours before and hours after everyone else had gone home. How much better will you be when you are coachable? How much easier will it be to achieve and live your dreams?

Eddie Robinson, the Gambling football coach, one of only four college coaches with over 400 wins, said, "Coaching is a profession of love. You can't coach them unless you love them." We don't consider how much time, effort, and love our teachers give us. We don't think or know about the hours they spend preparing their sessions, classes, or workshops. We don't consider the hours they invested in their own training, schooling, and education. We have no idea what they had to do to become a coach or teacher. Their hard work and dedication has come from love. When you stop to consider and comprehend the hard work and dedication that came from love, you become more coachable. When you understand your coach-coachee relationship from your coach's point of view, you are that much closer to living the life of your dreams.

The more coachable you become, the faster and easier you can achieve your dreams. When you begin to comprehend what your coaches are doing for you, you can more easily do everything your coach tells and guides you to do.

Coach

* a private tutor
* one who instructs or trains
* one who instructs players in the fundamentals of a sport

Merriam-Webster

Why Become Coachable?

This is a simple question to answer. Success. We all have an inert need to not only survive but to thrive. We are like that weed or blade of grass that somehow grows through the sidewalk. It was determined to make it, no matter what the obstacles. Our parents wanted us to have a better life than they had. We naturally want to be, do, and have more. If this wasn't built into our psyche, our DNA, the wheel, fire, or the Rubik's cube would have taken much longer to be invented.

The greatest part of having a coach is we don't have to invent anything new. Our coach has already been where we want to go. They have climbed that mountain, navigated that sea, tamed that lion. The roadmap has already been drawn, and your coach has already traversed that path. If you are coachable, you're already halfway to the life you desire. If you want to have a life that makes a difference, if you want to leave a legacy for the world, if you want to have, be, and do more...become coachable.

Finding Your Coach

Remember the Buddhist proverb, "When the student is ready, the teacher will appear." When you sincerely are ready to learn, to grow, to strive for your goals and dreams, your coach just might find you. Finding your coach is more about being ready than anything else. That's how it worked for me. When my coach, Dr. Reverend Joanne Coleman, saw me, she literally had a vision of my future life. She foresaw how I was to contribute to the world, how I was to make a difference. Rev. Joanne saw a vision of me and knew that helping me would help others.

Create an intention for yourself that you strongly desire to have a coach. There is a power in your intentionality. Dr. Wayne Dyer stated, "Our intention creates our reality." The first step is to determine what type of coach you want that will generate the greatest benefit. Who your coach will be depends on your dreams. If your dream is to play the piano, find a piano coach. One of my dreams was to play the Native American flute. I was looking for someone not only skilled and knowledgeable musically, but who also has a respect and appreciation of the culture of Native Americans. I also wanted a coach who has a spiritual nature that matches the spiritual nature of the flute.

I also took the action of making a phone call in the quest of finding that coach. Yes, it only took me one call. I called a Native American store called Four Crows. I simply asked, "Do you know of a flute teacher?" It so happened they were sponsoring a class that week. It was that easy! I found my coach. All it took was knowing who I was looking for, a little thought of where that person could be found, and a single phone call.

> *"Wax on. Wax off"*
> *~Mr. Miyagi,*
> *The Karate Kid*

Don't get discouraged if your search for a coach takes time. To be ready, you may need to clarify what your dream is so you can determine where you will most likely discover your perfect coach. Once you determine your dreams, you can begin by asking friends, relatives, and co-workers if they know a coach in that field, or if they would refer you to someone who does. Do some detective work. It will only be a matter of time before you find your coach. Be selective. The first coach you meet may not be the right one. See Chapter Eight "Follow Your Intuition" to give you insight to choosing your perfect coach.

Michelle can do several things to bring herself into position to find her coach to help her with her dream of owning a McDonald's franchise. Michelle can talk with managers and owners of different franchises and be around people who know of potential mentors and coaches specific for her dream.

As you start to meet potential coaches, check in with your intuition. How do you feel about this person? How do you relate with each other? Is there some common interests, in addition to your dream, that you both share? Look for someone you can relate to and with. Most of all, look into their heart. The right coach will love what they are doing. If they don't love what they are doing, keep looking.

> "I respect coaches; I respect what good coaches do. I know that you don't learn to be a coach in an hour and a half."
> ~John Madden

Why You Want to Have a Coach

Experience is the primary reason you have a coach. You want someone who has already traversed on your path. The right coach means you won't have to take nearly as many detours on the way to living your dreams. They will shorten your learning curve, thus making things much easier for you. Your coach will help you achieve your dreams perhaps years quicker than you could on your own.

The problem we often have as human beings is that we don't easily change our behaviors or habits on our own. "Doing the same thing over and expecting a different result," according to Einstein, "is the definition of insanity." My goal, to be a magnificent husband, is a perfect example. My approach to and toward women was always the same. I'm sorry to say, so were my results. My success will never change until I do. The best, easiest, and fastest method to change is with the assistance of a coach.

Where We Mess Up

We tend to take shortcuts toward our dreams. When we take shortcuts, we are almost always in conflict with our goals and dreams. We see the short-term satisfaction, and our mind overrides our desire for something greater in the future. Our priority for short-term satisfaction appears as a lack of motivation. Here are a few reasons one might not be motivated to have a coach:

1. A coach is too expensive.
2. I don't see the benefits.
3. I don't think he or she will help me.
4. I think I can do it myself.
5. It's boring.
6. I would rather invest my time doing something else.
7. My friends want me to hang out with them instead.
8. Working with a coach might not be fun.

We often do what we do because of consequences. The consequences could be negative or positive. Because of our desire to avoid pain and seek pleasure, we tend to prioritize short-term consequences over our long-term goals and dreams. With a short-term mentality, we figure, why should I do something if it's boring? We also don't want to engage in activities that aren't fun or where we possibly could look foolish. Peer pressure is another short-term consequence that encourages us to or not to do certain activities. We receive immediate positive reinforcement for going the easy route. If the activity is new to you, you may avoid it because of your desire to do it perfect from the beginning. It is also possible you could get attention for not engaging in a particular activity. My favorite excuse is that I think my unproven method is better. All of these are reasons you might choose not to even attempt to become coachable.

One of the biggest ways we are not coachable is that we don't do what our coach wants us to do. Some of them are:

1. Fear (we anticipate future negative consequences)
2. Perceived personal limitations
3. Personal problems
4. You don't know <u>how</u> to do it.
5. You don't know <u>what</u> you are supposed to do.
6. You don't know <u>when</u> to do it.
7. You don't know <u>why</u> you should do it.
8. You think it will not work.
9. You think your way is better.
10. You think something else is more important.
11. There are no positive consequences for doing it.
12. There are no negative consequences for not doing it.
13. There is a positive consequence for not doing it.

It boils down to laying the groundwork with the what, how, when, and why you are in the coaching/coachee relationship to begin with. If you have your goals and dreams constantly in mind and are consistent and honest, you will be motivated to do what your coach instructs you to do.

Often, you leave it up to your coach to do all the work for you. Your parents did everything for you when you were an infant. You were trained that someone else can do it for you. Without your effort, dedication, and hard work, even the best coach in the world will not be able to assist you to reach your dreams. Only when you are willing to do whatever it takes can you live the life you want, the life of your dreams.

Make Sure You Understand

What is it exactly that your coach wants you to do? Clear and accurate understanding is a problem many of us have. A problem is often with having the courage to ask for clarity, especially for men. A man's ego doesn't want to appear foolish, ignorant, or less than perfect. Have you noticed, most men will never ask for directions even when totally lost? A man's ego simply won't allow it. Whether you are a man or a woman, not asking for clarity on what your coach is saying isn't helping your coach, coach you. If you don't say anything, your coach believes you understand. Make sure you understand completely. Don't be afraid to simply ask a question. Remember, there really is no dumb question. As Og Mandino stated, "Take the attitude of a student. Never be too big to ask questions. Never know too much to learn something new."

Catch your dreams

Understanding

* a mental grasp
* the power of comprehending
* the power to make experience intelligible by applying concepts and categories

Merriam-Webster

Your coach will appreciate you when you do ask questions. It will show you have an interest in understanding the instructions. The question shows you care enough to find out exactly what your coach wants you to do. Your questions demonstrate interest and motivation. John Whitmore, in his book *Coach for Performance,* said, "I'm able to control only that which I'm aware of. That of which I'm unaware controls me." If you don't ask, you are unaware and are not utilizing your coach to the fullest. Even if you think you understand the request, it's best to paraphrase the statement back to your coach for clarity. Asking for clarity is one of the best things you can do to become coachable.

Don't allow your ego to get in your way. Speak up and don't be timid. Be yourself. Don't try to be something that you are not. The more you are yourself, the better your coach can work with you. The better your coach knows you, the better she can instruct, guide, and explain things to you. If you are not authentic and honest, you won't have a chance to be coachable. Take good notes, and rephrase the assignments back to your coach for clear understanding.

The most important thing you can do to become coachable is to be 100% cooperative with your coach. Listen, pay attention, and understand what your coach is talking about. Be open-minded to whatever the or she asks you to do. For instance, Mr. Miygai in *The Karate Kid* had Daniel wax his cars, sand the floor, and paint the fence. Each chore gave Daniel practice with a karate movement. Repetition is how we learn things. As the great Napoleon Hill shared, "Any idea, plan, or purpose may be placed in the mind through repetition of thought."

My coach, Rev. Joanne, likes to use the Dr. Phil phrase,"How's that working for you?" Without a coach, there is no one to give you honest feedback. There is no one to tell you, you are on the right or wrong track. I believe for many, our egos feel as if having a coach implies you are not whole. Your ego thinks you must have something missing within you to need a coach. The ego thinks you should be perfect, you should be an expert, you should understand what to do, even when doing something for the first time. Knowing how to do something perfectly for the first time is not realistic, and honestly, leaves little room for learning or creativity.

With a coach you can learn and know new things that would be nearly impossible to learn on your own. How is your progress toward your dreams? How has not having a coach been working for you? If you are doing things you have never done, it is normal not to be perfect. If you want to be an expert overnight, or ever, you need a coach.

Your coach must also have the expertise of teaching. You are looking for someone who knows the subject, can be your friend, and has the skills to teach it to you. Being a friend, knowing the subject and the skill to teach it, is the triune nature of coaching. When you are looking for your coach, make sure to ask them, "How has it been working for you?"

Learn to Listen

Your mind is constantly reacting to outside stimulus. If I say, "red" most people will think of blue. If I say, "up" your mind will react and most likely think down. These two are examples of how you can be reactive. When your coach is saying "up," your coach wants your mind to think up and not down. The goal in listening is to hear what was actually said and not allow your mind to wander.

Keep an open mind and relax into not thinking so much. Surrender to trusting, and be fully engaged in the moment. It's time that you realize there is a method to your coach's madness. Be fully and completely trusting and open with as little mental questioning in your mind as possible.

We want to be independent. I used to play men's slow pitch softball. I would be playing left field, and the shortstop Larry and left center fielder Chris would tell me where to position myself depending on their thoughts on where the batter most likely would hit the ball. The problem is that my ego said I wanted to stand where I guessed where the batter most likely would hit the ball. I believed I had a better guess on where the opposing batter would hit the ball than Larry or Chris. Then I thought that maybe Larry or Chris might have as good a guess or even better guess than I did. They both were more experienced, therefore they would have more knowledge of the game and possibly the individual batter. When I finally surrendered to their advice, they both noticed and were happily surprised at my willingness to follow their advice. This experience helped me in learning about becoming coachable. Think of it like the old TV show *Father Knows Best*. In your life you can call it, *My Coach Knows Best.*

"Your pain is the breaking of the shell that encloses your understanding."
~Khalil Gibran

John Whitmore shared from his book, *Coaching for Performance*, "If we don't change direction, we are liable to end up where we are headed." You do want to change because where you are headed may not be where you want to go. Obviously, on your own, you may or may not be headed in the right direction. The best way to know where to go is to seek the assistance of, and listen to, someone who knows how to get there.

As mentioned in the last chapter, "Charting Your Dreams", you won't get anywhere without a chart. A smart ship captain won't take his ship out until he knows exactly where he wants his ship to go. He will listen to his navigator

and chart a course based on the information. You can't reach your destination unless you know where you are going. The right coach has been there and done that. It is up to you to hear what your coach tells you.

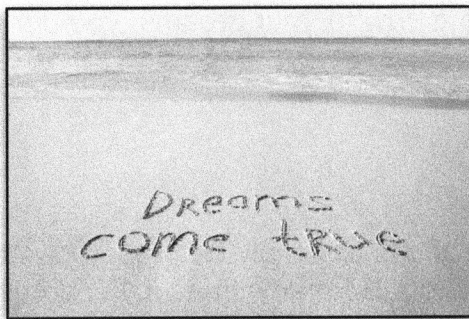

Communication

* the imparting or exchanging of information or news

* means of connection between people or places

Source: Merriam-Webster

Vow to be Coachable

A vow is sacred. It is a promise, an oath, to keep one's word. A vow declares, "I'm going to do it." With a vow such as marriage, we promise to cherish, love, and be true to another person. Why not make a vow to be true to your coach and your dreams? A vow is your solemn promise, your word. I love the old Western days (at least on TV) where they didn't sign legal documents; they gave their word.

One of the functions of your coach is to hold you accountable, to make sure you follow the vows you made to yourself, your coach, and to your dreams. Make that promise, put it in writing, sign, and date it (see appendix #5). Have the pride, and honor, and take the responsibility to complete your vows. You may have a tendency to fight your coach. I know for me, I often unknowingly and unwittingly sabotage myself by not honoring my vows or promises I make with my coach.

When you make a vow to yourself, your coach, and your dreams, magnificent and amazing things will begin to happen. Tasks will get done more easily. You will meet the right people. Resources will seem to come out of nowhere to assist you.

I love what Yoda, one of the Jedi coaches from *Star Wars,* said, "Don't try, do. There is no try, either you do or you don't." When you make a vow to your dreams, you don't try, you do.

Support Your Coach

One way to support your coach is to simply be prepared and ready for your coaching session. So many times my coach in high school would go to the baseball field for practice, and myself and many of my teammates didn't even have our shoes on yet. John Wooden, the legendary coach from UCLA, spent three hours of preparation for every one hour of practice. Coach Wooden devoted so much to his players, and he demanded by his devotion, the devotion of his players. Their devotion to each other and Coach Wooden resulted in eleven NCCA championships! Coach Wooden devoted six hours of preparation for a two-hour practice. The eleven championships demonstrate his players were ready.

Value your coach; be ready; have an open mind; leave your reactive, argumentative mind at home. Be willing and eager to do whatever is asked. In other words, do anything and everything your coach asks you to. As in my softball example, be willing to stand wherever your coach asks you to stand.

Be an open vessel to achieve your dreams. Allow your coach to coach, and to even love you. Let him or her know you appreciate all that they do. Do something for them. You can start by honoring your vows. By taking the time to think about what your coach does for you, it will help you comprehend their value. You may begin to remember that they are invaluable.

Imagine if you were to try and buy a McDonald's franchise, earn your GED, or become a magnificent husband totally on your own. How much would it be worth to you if you knew someone who knew all the details, someone who knows the best path for you to assist you to achieve your dreams? You wouldn't have to run over the bumpy road and take a thousand detours along the way. How much would that be worth? What is a guide who knows the way worth? Appreciate and support your coach. If you have the right coach, they are supporting and appreciating you.

Have Confidence

Confidence seems rather simple and easy. For some to be confident is only natural, but for many it is very elusive. I'm talking specifically about having the confidence to speak up and be yourself. Your coach needs to know exactly what you are thinking, feeling, and doing so they can best help you. Having the confidence to know and say what is on your mind is imperative for clear communication between you and your coach.

For me, speaking up has been a major challenge. I have been afraid that if I speak up, I won't be liked, approved of, or worst of all, I might be considered stupid. I had the misconception that being liked, accepted, and not to be considered stupid was my major goal in life. In truth, I couldn't stand the thought of rejection, real or imagined. Trying to get everyone to like me made sense to me. I learned the hard way that placing my attention on being liked ruined any chance of clear and honest communication. You need the confidence and courage to speak up, to express your feelings, goals, and dreams. Without knowing your feelings, goals, and dreams, your coach has little chance of helping you.

To gain confidence you can start by knowing you will survive if you aren't liked by everyone. Life will go on, and saying what's on your mind actually feels good. Taking care and honoring yourself is healthy. To gain confidence, you can stop to realize how special you are. There is no one else who is like you, no one. You have special and unique gifts to offer the world. You were made in the image and likeness of our creator. You have the ability to think, to reason, to problem solve. Take the time and realize how amazing it is to be you.

Stay Interested

Stay interested in the process of living your dreams. It's not that difficult when all you have to do is conduct a Google search regarding your dreams. You can read about it, study it on YouTube, and talk about your dreams. Share your dreams to your family, friends, co-workers, and neighbors. Tell the person at the supermarket, pharmacy, or local restaurant about your dreams. When you generate interest in others, you'll generate interest in it for yourself. In sharing and enrolling others in your passions, you will fall deeper in love with your dreams.

Be enthusiastic, make it a game, make it fun to stay interested and focused on your dreams. Your dream should be something that deeply matters to you. You should actually dream, and daydream about your dreams most all the time.

As kids, we were discouraged and often punished for daydreaming. I'm telling you to daydream. I'm saying for you to constantly think about and visualize yourself fully engaged in your dreams. The more you visualize in vivid detail, the better chance and the faster you will realize your dreams. The important thing for you to realize your dreams is to stay interested.

Dream Notes

To Jump-Start Your Dreams

Spend some time in nature this week. Take a walk in a park, in the mountains or at the beach.

Don't Take It Personally

I'm not excited about receiving criticism. Criticism often makes me feel like there is something wrong with me. To me, criticism says that I'm not good enough. Your coach is not out to hurt and discourage you. Your coach is teaching, instructing, directing, and hoping to transform your dreams into your reality.

When you keep your eye on your dreams, it is easier to see what can be perceived as criticism as positive instructions rather than disparagement. You can understand criticism as a means of feedback for you to reach your dreams. Your coach is just helping you with a course correction. For example, if you are learning to play the guitar, your coach might simply show you where your fingers go. It is easy to understand this instruction, and a finger adjustment isn't an indictment on you personally.

I like to think of my coach's instructions as if my coach isn't talking to me, but talking to that part of me that is unaware and in need of a course correction. My coach is talking to that guy, not to that part of me who takes things personally. When you remember it isn't about you personally, it makes it easier to listen to instructions.

Your coach has experience and expertise on getting you from where you are to where you want to be. They are simply helping you reach your dreams. Your coach isn't trying to hurt your feelings. If you keep in mind your coach's good intentions, the next time you receive instructions you won't be hurt by them. Receiving criticism, or instructions, doesn't mean there is anything wrong with you. The feedback you receive is given with the intention of simply helping you get to where you want to go.

We are all human and thus imperfect, as humans we are just learning and will continue to learn as there is an infinite amount of information available. With an infinite amount to learn, by definition we will never know everything there is to know. The problem is sometimes our ego doesn't want to admit that we don't know everything. There is a great example in the book *The Inner Game of Tennis* by Timothy Galloway. In the book, Galloway has an example of a coach asking a student if he watched the ball. The student, not wanting to admit they don't really know, lied and said, "Yes." Then the coach asked, "Which way was the ball spinning?" The student had no idea what direction the ball was spinning, and that wasn't an insult. It was just a point that Galloway was making to help his student to improve. If you refuse to take instruction personally, you will reach your dreams more easily.

"You see things, and you say,
'Why?' But I dream things
that never were, and I say,
'Why not?'"
~George Bernard Shaw

Dazzle Your Coach

It is easy when you can see the value of your coach. If you knew what nature had to do in making a diamond or a pearl, you could more easily understand the value of your coach. Learn about your coach's education, experience, and track record. Find out your coach's level of commitment they are giving to help you. They may be making and changing plans to accommodate your schedule. You coach may be taking less money, getting up extra early, or fighting a physical challenge you are unaware of. Comprehending the true value of your coach will motivate you to dazzle them.

You dazzle your coach by simply making progress in the realization of your dreams. Go for it. Do everything that they tell you to do. You can dazzle your coach by following their instructions exactly as given. You dazzle your coach by doing something extra, by showing up early and staying late. You dazzle your coach by loving your dreams and ultimately loving yourself.

Don Shula and Ken Blounch in their book, *Everyone's a Coach,* wrote about a method to dazzle your coach by this statement: "A change in behavior, you haven't learned a thing until you take action." Dazzle your coach by doing something different. Take action, be enthusiastic, go beyond what is asked, be timely and ready for your meetings. Mia Hamm, the great American soccer player, is a great example. Mia went the extra mile. She kicked more balls, ran more laps, lifted more weights, and followed exactly what her coaches told her. Joe Paterno, the head coach of Penn State for over forty-six years, said, "The will to win is important, but the willingness to prepare is vital." Sheila McKeithen, who teaches high integrity at the Agape International Spiritual Center, teaches us to honor our word, to do what we say, and honor our commitments.

Major Points to Be a Great Coachee

1. Ask questions when you don't understand.
2. Be appreciative and remember all your coach has done.
3. Be available and ready to do everything your coach says.
4. Be prepared and ready early for each meeting.
5. Communicate by asking questions.
6. Comprehend the brilliance of your coach.
7. Consider all of the classes, workshops, books they have read, all the monies spent for their education.
8. Consider their talents and all the hats your coach has to wear to assist you.
9. Remember your coach is working for you and your dreams.
10. Make sure you know exactly what is intended for you to do.
11. Pay attention and get your reactive mind out of the way.
12. Stay excited, enthusiastic, motivated, and in love with your dreams.
13. Stay on track and in integrity.

Your coach is a counselor, psychologist, teacher, friend, communicator, psychic, and a cheerleader for you. Remember all the preparation they do for you, like John Wooden who spent three hours for every one hour of practice. Your coach has chosen you as much as you have chosen them, so go out and dazzle them and be coachable.

The most successful people in history all had a coach and obviously learned how to be coachable. Michael Jordan was coached by Phil Jackson and Norm Smith at North Carolina. The Greek philosopher Plato was mentored by Socrates. Helen Keller was tutored by Annie Sullivan. Knowing how successful they all were, consider the effort, hard work and cooperation they must have given to their coaches. You know they did everything their coach requested and more.

Conclusion

Michael Jordan, the greatest basketball player of all time, had Phil Jackson as a coach. Meryl Streep, one of the greatest actors of all time, has had many coaches. It is easy to understand, if you want to get to the top of the mountain, ask someone who has already been to the top, someone who has been there and done that.

There is more to catching your dreams than having a coach. You must be coachable. Michael Jordan didn't just go onto the basketball floor, grab four guys, and go win six championships. He followed the coaching of Phil Jackson. I'm sure at first glance, Michael wasn't sure about Phil's now-famous triangle offense. Michael was willing to give this new way of attacking a defense a try, to learn it, and perfect himself within it. And there are six world championships, five times as the MVP of the National Basketball Association, fourteen all-star appearances, and two Olympic gold medals to prove Mr. Jordan was indeed quite coachable.

The first step in being coachable is to see, understand, and hear the value in being coachable. You are not Michael Jordan, and you can be the best you, you can be. You will not be the best you can be without a coach and without you being coachable. You deserve to live the life of your dreams, and you are sure to catch your dreams when you are coachable.

"It's what you learn after you know it all that counts."
~John Wooden

DREAMS
COME
TRUE

Recap — Become Coachable

Why Become Coachable? you become coachable in order to succeed.

Finding Your Coach: be ready, have an intention, and take the necessary action.

Why You Want to Have a Coach: you learn from their experience.

Where We Mess Up: we don't appreciate the value that a coach gives us.

Make Sure Your Understand: make sure you know what your coach wants you to do.

Learn to Listen: pay attention to what is actually said.

Vow to be Coachable: make a promise to your coach and yourself.

Support Your Coach: be on time and ready.

Have Confidence: speak up, be yourself, and let your coach know how best they can assist you.

Stay Interested: be enthusiastic and in love with your dreams.

Don't Take It Personally: be willing to receive criticism and feedback.

Dazzle Your Coach: do something extra; go for your dreams 100%.

Dreamtime
Do Try This at Home

1. If you don't already have a coach, get one. Ask everyone you know. Call successful people in the area of your dreams. When all else fails, go to the ultimate source. Use Google to find your coach.

2. Schedule an appointment with your coach.

3. Be sure you know exactly what your coach instructs you to do. Repeat all assignments, homework, or exercises back to your coach.

4. Put your assignments on a wall, bathroom mirror, and the refrigerator. Put them in your special notebook just for your assignments.

5. Read your assignments daily.

6. What extra thing can you do this week? Invest at least five minutes and write down as many ideas as you can, and then this week act on at least two.

7. Write a vow or promise to you and your coach to Become
   Coachable (see appendix #5).

_____

_____

_____

_____

_____

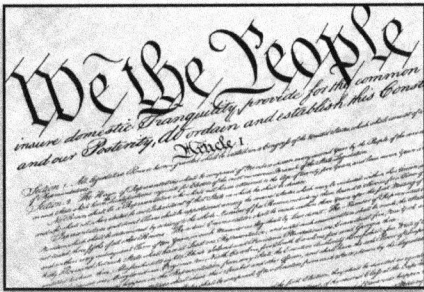

Declaration: From today onward, I will do
whatever my coach instructs me to do.

Your

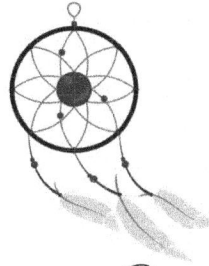

DREAM CATCHER

Chapter IV. Transform the Heckler Into Your Hero

"Only through love, transformation of the so-called wicked ones is possible."

~Sri Sathya Si Baba

You need not remain a prisoner in a self-made jail with no bars. Even a villain from within can be transformed. Out of your deepest fears and from your most devious interior enemies, there is hope. You can live the life of your dreams. The yearning from your heart is the foundation for your liberation. It is never too late.

The villain within is what I call the Heckler. The Heckler is a mean-spirited inner voice that continually recites, "This is too difficult!" "I'll never learn to do that!" "I'm not good enough or smart enough!" The Heckler is a belief that repeatedly shouts, "I'm not worthy! I'll never be as good as my father, mother, brother, or sister!" Hecklers are feelings and an inner voice that convinces you that you are not good, smart, or talented enough to catch your dreams.

On a Mission-Not from God

One of the Heckler's missions is to protect you from embarrassment, shame, or even the thought of failure. The Heckler guards you from any possibility of failure by discouraging you from attempting new activities, events, projects, or dreams. The idea is that nothing ventured insures no failures. The Heckler has many faces, but one objective, to stop you dead in your tracks! The Heckler paralyzes you with the cold chill of unworthiness. He/she uses a false sense of low self-esteem to stifle even the thought of moving forward in your life.

Disguised as a caring inner voice, the Heckler tricks you into believing its messages to be what's best for you. The Heckler is similar to a fanatical sports fan screaming at a player from the opposing team. They attempt to distract, discourage, and trick the athlete into performing poorly. Hecklers attempt to humiliate and embarrass standup comedians. The Heckler attempts to display to the entire audience that the comedian has little or no talent and isn't a bit funny. Unlike the seasoned athlete or comedian, we often believe the Heckler's rants. Hearing a rant, such as, "You aren't good enough," and, "You're a bum" over and over, ultimately and tragically can become your reality.

The Heckler never rests. As children we needed an adult to guard and protect us. At one time it wasn't safe to cross the street by ourselves, or prepare and cook our own meals. We were forbidden to talk to strangers. We weren't savvy enough to even pick out our own clothes. As adults, it's nearly impossible to achieve your dreams if you can't cross the street or meet anyone new. Until you transform the Heckler into your hero, you are still being distracted, disconnected, and discouraged from your dreams. As adults, the Heckler is no longer necessary to protect you. You can decide for yourself what is safe and what may be dangerous.

Catch your dreams

Hero

* a mythological or legendary figure
* a person admired for achievements and noble qualities
* one who shows great courage

Merriam-Webster

The Heckler's objective is to protect you from making mistakes, looking like a fool, and being laughed at. They block your dreams by reminding you of times in your life where you tripped up, fell down, mumbled, or did anything less than perfectly. The Heckler uses any method it can to discourage you, from embarrassment, shame, or believing you have failed in any way. The Heckler reasons that if you don't try, you don't fail. If you don't do anything new or challenging, you will be protected. The shame of repeating the offense is often all that's necessary to destroy your dreams.

The Heckler has a flawless memory. It remembers, exaggerates, and adds details regarding all of your mishaps, real or imagined. Their database contains the times you tripped, fell down, became tongue-tied, got laughed at or criticized. The Heckler uses your past to stop your progress today. The Heckler's prime directive is to defend you from any additional similar situations.

The Voice

The voice in our head projects negativity and fear to control you. Rick Carson from his book, *Taming Your Gremlins,* describes the voice when he wrote, "He tells you who and how you are, and he defines and interprets your every experience. He wants you to accept his interpretations as reality, and his goal, from moment to moment, day to day, is to squelch the natural, vibrant you within." The Heckler's bag of tricks includes doubt, worry, negative thinking, and pessimistic self-talk. The Heckler encourages you to dread your past and worry about your future. He shames and frightens you into not doing anything that may resemble a risk.

My Heckler used fictional characters to manipulate me! The best example is the character Jethro Bodine, played by Max Baer, from the 1960s television show *The Beverly Hillbillies.* I snickered at Jethro's childlike innocence and unfamiliarity with his new life as a Beverly Hills millionaire. I laughed at him and his phobias, and at the same time identified with the miscues of the character. I was simultaneously the laugher and the laughee. I laughed at Jethro while projecting the shame of his ignorance on myself. The fear of appearing childlike, ignorant, or unsophisticated propelled me to hide much of my personality. The Heckler made sure I was continuously aware of my connection with Jethro.

The Heckler uses a plethora of tricks, sayings, rants, and distractions to lure you into a misguided sanctuary of safety (see appendix #3), a refuge with no goals, purpose, or dreams, an asylum that we must escape to live the lives we dream of.

I See You

Awareness of the Heckler is your first step toward freedom. This chapter will give you the information and understanding to detect the Heckler's behaviors, rants, and directives. You will then recognize the heckling as a signal of where you need to grow, not as an additional area you must avoid. They simply point out areas of your life where more clarity is needed. The Heckler identifies aspects of your life that require more information, training, or advice. The moment you start to use the Heckler's remarks as guides to grow, rather than an excuse to stop or procrastinate, you have transformed the Heckler into your hero.

> "A hero is someone who has given his or her life to something bigger than oneself."
> ~Joseph Campbell

The Heckler-Your Inner Critic

Hecklers can masquerade as your inner voice, a feeling, thought, amnesia, depression, numbness, or a distraction. They induce you into procrastination, confusion, overwhelm, and avoidance. Hecklers trick you into doing anything other than moving toward your goals and dreams. Your inner Heckler, or critic, knows exactly what buttons to push to interrupt and stifle you. Even your smallest movements toward your dreams are prey to the Heckler.

Criticism is the Heckler's favorite weapon. He says you are no good, a has-been, a never-was, and that you can't get anything right. The fear of public humiliation, shame, and embarrassment is skillfully interwoven into the Heckler's rants. They convince you the only way to make sure you won't be made fun of, laughed at, humiliated, or look like a fool is to, **not even try. Ever!**

The Heckler functions the same as an automatic loop in a computer program. Every time you start something new, challenging, or creative, the sabotaging cycle is activated. The program continues until the day you consciously decide to shut it down.

One of my goals and dreams is for you to transform your Heckler into your Hero. It is my desire for you to live to your fullest potential. I don't want you to suffer the years and decades of frustration, shame, and unfulfilled dreams I did. I want you to achieve your dreams and live the life you dream of. I want you to be, Your Dream Catcher.

You can start to transform your Heckler by understanding the Heckler's behaviors, characteristics, and prime-directives (see appendix #1). I strongly encourage you to make copies and post them up in your home and carry a copy with you. Read them often. Memorize them so you will easily recognize them when they surface. When you finish this chapter and play with the Dreamtime exercises, you will be able to convert the Heckler's criticisms into constructive dream-enhancing activities. They will no longer be a catalyst leading you to procrastination or quitting on your dreams. They will be a signal to show you where you need more information, teaching, or attention. The next topic covers a few of the Heckler's tricks and techniques.

The Heckler's Stealth Mode

Your inner Heckler works discreetly and quietly under your conscious radar. Much of the time you don't notice them as the voice in your head. You believe the voice to be your own natural self doing the talking.

Here are a few of the times when it's your inner Heckler doing the talking:

- Anytime you procrastinate on your life and dreams.
- At the times you feel unorganized, frustrated, disoriented, lost, overwhelmed, sick, tired, shameful, embarrassed, not worthy, guilty, or confused.
- When for no reason you just don't feel like it.
- When you are easily distracted or do something completely different.
- When you intensify the work you are doing, making it more complicated and difficult.
- When you plan to work on a project and choose to do something else.
- When you rationalize why you are not moving toward your goals and dreams.
- Whenever you refuse to put goals and dreams on paper.
- When you talk yourself out of working toward your dreams. For example, rather than moving toward your dreams, you talk yourself into watching television, going to the movies, checking emails, playing with Facebook, or calling a friend. You reason with yourself that you will do it later.

Your inner Heckler uses stealth to its advantage. It isn't as obvious as a Heckler in a crowd yelling insults at a speaker, athlete, or comedian. We think it is our own inner voice talking. It seems to ring true and in your best interest to follow the advice or instructions you hear.

Now that you understand and can be conscious of this trick and many of the things to look out for, it is possible to expose your Heckler. Once you can spot and see through the Heckler's ploy, it will be much easier to say no. Once you say no, do something, anything that moves you toward your dreams, that tells the Heckler he or she is no longer necessary.

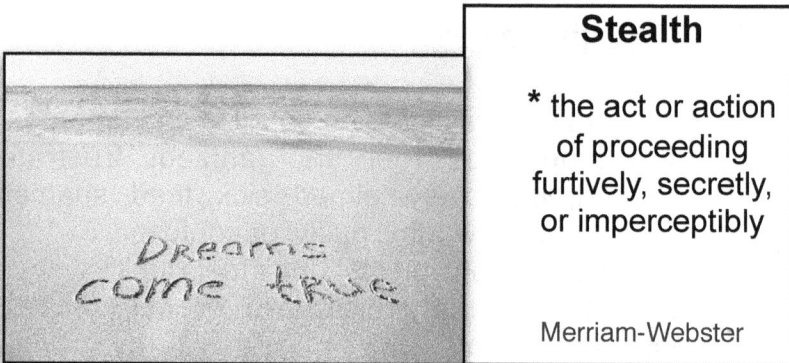

Stealth

* the act or action of proceeding furtively, secretly, or imperceptibly

Merriam-Webster

The Shame, Blame, Guilt Game

The Heckler persuades you to primarily dwell on your negative, shame-based, and self-critical nature. It injects pessimism, shame, blame, and guilt into your thoughts. An example of the shame, blame, guilt game could be when you awkwardly answered a teacher's question in grade school. When a few of the kids laughed, the voice in your head, (the Heckler) convinced you it was all about you. You believed the laughter was about how dumb, uncoordinated, or foolish you were.

The Heckler seized that opportunity to instill a fear of:

• Asking questions
• Public speaking
• Speaking up

The real truth about the laughter in the class may have been the result of the kids being caught off guard by the answer. The response may have been a bit personal or complex. It would be natural for the kids to laugh to relieve the tension of their own misunderstanding, or to laugh because of the intimacy of the question.

Hecklers make you feel sick and tired enough to forget about your commitments. They keep us unorganized, busy, overwhelmed, shy, and distracted. Your dreams and goals become unimportant or, sadly, often forgotten. The Heckler manipulates small amounts of information to trick you into engaging in misguided, unproductive activities. They use just enough of the truth to make the lies seem reasonable. Often we go completely blank, forgetting all about our commitments to our dreams.

The Heckler particularly likes to use shame, humiliation, laughter, and fear of criticism to thwart your progress. In the section below is an example that happened to me.

> "The future belongs to those who believe in the beauty of their dreams."
> ~ Eleanor Roosevelt

Our Childhood Stories

I will never forget my Aunt Debbie's wedding. I was seven years old. Mom bought me my first real grown-up suit just for the occasion. The suit fit perfectly; the shirt and tie were an exact match. My shoes were shined; my socks and belt were brand new. I thought I was about the hottest seven-year-old ever. The wedding was just about to start when Mom asked me to turn around on top of the podium in front of everyone to show off how handsome I looked.

That's when it happened. I tripped and fell. It was one of those slow-motion experiences where you remember every detail and are in control of none, the kind of incident where you grab whatever you can reach on the way down to most certain humiliation. I knocked over an arrangement of flowers, a small table, and bumped into a couple of chairs. Just in case there might be someone who didn't see me falling, I sent out a kind of scream on the way down. Not like a seven-year-old young man, but more like a little girl's high-pitched scream. In case there might be someone who didn't hear me, my mother also screamed, "Oooooooh, NOOOOOOOOOO."

By the time I knocked everything over and settled at the bottom of the steps, there they were, all one hundred people staring at me. The music and all conversation stopped. I might as well have been Merrill Lynch, with nothing to say. This was a moment frozen in time and etched in my memory. After a few moments of complete and absolute silence...that seemed to last forever, a silence intensified by those 200 focused eyes glaring at me, I didn't know what to do. I wished I was invisible.

My family and all of their friends gathered even closer. I collected myself the best I could. I seemed to be fine -- no broken bones, or major bruises. There was a hint of blood seeping through a tear at the left knee of my pants. Otherwise, I seemed to be unhurt. I knew I couldn't disappear so I decided to get up so I could hastily get away and hide. It's a decision I regret to this day. It seemed like all I could do at the time. In hindsight, if I could do it over, I would have just lain there and let someone pick me up and carry me away as fast as possible. Then I wouldn't have experienced the additional embarrassment and shame.

As I stood up, the crowd realized I wasn't hurt. Unexplainably to me, they all began laughing, and laughing, and laughing some more. It seemed like they would never stop, and in my heart they never have. If only I could have disappeared. To make matters worse, my mother made a huge deal of it. She bragged over me, saying, "Davie is such a cute young stunt man," and "He is an athlete like his older brother, rolling down those steps and not getting hurt." There was nowhere to go, nowhere to hide. I was totally and completely humiliated. In my memory I can still hear everyone laughing, and laughing.

The Heckler was created to guard you from those kinds of situations.

They speak to you in the first person, saying things like:

- "I don't ever want to be in front of a group of people again."
- "I'll never get dressed up again."
- "I'll do anything to avoid being laughed at again."
- "I'm so uncoordinated, I can't do anything right."
- "It's my mother's fault."
- "Nobody likes me."
- "They all hate me."
- "They laughed because I'm a fool."

The Heckler uses its superb memory to make sure, no matter what, nothing similar happens again. You avoid attention. Stop asking questions. Stick faithfully to only what you know. You do as little as possible. There is no way you will ever again try anything for the first time or take any risks.

The Heckler also persuades you to continue looking at these events (your stories) through the eyes and perspective of a child and/or victim. Your adult, more sensible self is not consulted. An adult perspective could understand why people might laugh for reasons other than to simply humiliate you. In my mind, I have reenacted this story as that seven-year-old for over fifty years. Could it be that the Heckler influenced me to think and to continue to remember this story from an uninformed viewpoint?

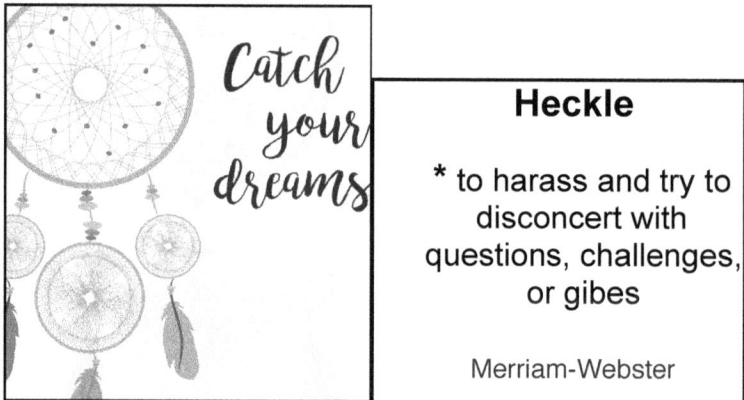

Catch your dreams

Heckle

* to harass and try to disconcert with questions, challenges, or gibes

Merriam-Webster

What if you could find a way to retell your stories, told from a fresh perspective, one that no longer needs the Heckler to guard you? My story goes back to how I thought of myself as a child, back to how I believed the world looked and responded to me. Like most kids, I obsessed about what others thought about me. I made up all kinds of negative, false, and exaggerated stories about their opinions of me and my own opinions of myself.

Now I can look at the fall from an entirely different viewpoint, free from the Heckler's influence, when I was lying on the ground about to get up, rather than experience the humiliation and shame of those 200 eyes. What my little David couldn't know, I could know today. I can now comprehend what they were really thinking, feeling, and experiencing. Now I know that the guests and friends didn't gather and rush to me to make fun of me. I realize they were simply concerned for my welfare.

Laughter is simply a release of tension. This fact is brought into light in *Communication World*, Oct.-Nov. 1998. James P.T. Fatt commented about Sigmund Freud saying, "Freud considered laughter as a way of releasing nervous energy because it provides relief and self-gratification and renders potentially damaging conflicts harmless."
This is precisely what happened. When the adults discovered I wasn't hurt, they were relieved. Their laughing was a means of releasing nervous energy caused by my fall. They were gratified to know that I wasn't hurt, relieved that a possibly dangerous fall turned out to be harmless. Naturally they all laughed. Their laughter was an automatic response to the situation.

> "Dream as if you'll live forever; live as if you'll die today."
> ~James Dean

Laughter is also contagious. When the laughter started, it multiplied and continued. As Robert Provine, Ph.D., stated in a special to MSNBC, "Laughter is social and contagious. We laugh at the sound of laughter itself. That's why the Tickle Me Elmo doll was such a success--it makes us laugh and smile." My fall turned out to be a Tickle Me Elmo moment.

As an adult with this understanding, I can now see a more realistic and accurate story, not my seven-year-old version. With a broader understanding, I can be happy that the guests were concerned for me. I can finally get in front of a group without feeling terrified. I feel comfortable dressing up. I'm not so self-conscious. I no longer pray that I won't be laughed at. Now when I meet resistance, I realize that is a guide revealing something I need to work on. At that moment I recognize it as a friend telling me simply where I need more attention. At that moment the Heckler has been transformed into my hero.

To help me recognize and transform the Heckler, I imagine it to be the fictional character Eddie Haskell. He played a major supporting role on the *Leave it the Beaver* television show. Jerry Mathers starred, playing the eight- to fourteen-year-old Beaver Cleaver. He lived with his parents June and Ward Cleaver and older brother Wally. Eddie Haskell was Wally's best friend, played by the actor Ken Osmond.

Eddie is a perfect example of the Heckler. His insecurities within himself caused him to do everything he could to interrupt and inject negativity into Beaver's life. By keeping Beaver's life small, Eddie felt better about his own insignificant life. As Beaver would say, "That Eddie is a rat."

Eddie Haskell was tall, slim, and good-looking. He had a persistent, wide, devilish grin. His curly dark blond hair was always neatly cut and combed. He was, without fail, impeccably dressed, with perfectly tailored and pressed pants and shirt. He was excessively polite and courteous to Mr. and Mrs. Cleaver. Eddie overstated his accomplishments, criticized, and put others down. Eddie loved to talk Beaver into doing things that got him into trouble.

By being overly polite to adults Eddie attempted to camouflage his mischievous deeds, manipulation, and outright lies. Eddie tried to get in good with the Cleavers so they would allow him to meddle in Beaver's life. His two-faced style was typified by how he spoke extra polite to Mr. and Mrs. Cleaver. He used the formal names Theodore (Beaver's much-disliked given name) and Wallace, even though the Cleavers called them Beaver and Wally.

Eddie did to Beaver what the Heckler does to us. Eddie often would discourage Beaver from his goals and dreams. More likely Eddie would coax Beaver into trouble by convincing Beaver into doing things without his parents' knowledge or permission. Beaver believed Eddie's advice was the best choice, given the circumstances. Later after he got into trouble, Beaver would realize Eddie seemed to continuously sabotage his life. Beaver explained how Eddie could talk him into poor decisions, saying, "Eddie makes stupid stuff sound smart."

Eddie wasn't a bad kid; he just had extremely poor methods for handling his insecurities. Eddie would feel better about himself by maneuvering Beaver into trouble. By keeping Beaver's life small, Eddie felt better about his own.

The Heckler is similarly detrimental and damaging to your life. It's important to understand that we have our own Eddie or Edith heckling us. They are capable of blocking even our memories of our goals and dreams. Regrettably, we don't realize it's the Heckler who persuades us to watch TV, check emails, surf the Internet, make phone calls, read the paper, and thus forget all about our commitment to our dreams.

Amazingly, we don't blame the Heckler for ruining our plans, goals, and dreams. We are often satisfied living our small, unproductive, uneventful lives. If we do feel the need to assign accountability, we blame ourselves or often our parents! We forget we are adults. We don't realize how the inner Heckler conspired against us. We blame, belittle, and put ourselves down for our lack of progress, focus, and organization. We end up conditioned to believe it's best not to try anything challenging in the future.

By beating ourselves up, we become more frustrated, overwhelmed, disorganized, busy, often sick, and for sure tired. The Heckler successfully prevents us from desiring or even thinking about another dance, another class, business, lover, project, vacation, home, or dream.

Dream Notes

To Jump-Start Your Dreams

Post pictures of your Dreams where you can see them-every day.

Hecklers Create Failure

I recall an example demonstrating how truly devious the Heckler can be. This incident occurred when I was in college. It was about three in the afternoon at the end of the last day of school. Knowing it would be my last chance, I ventured to a girl's dorm room. I wasn't sure, but I believed her name to be Jackie. I walked across campus with the hope to get her phone number, a date, and then Jackie would become my girlfriend.

My inner Heckler actually encouraged me to go! It knew something I didn't want to admit, that there was very little chance for my success. I knew very little about this girl, and she knew less about me. I had no idea where she lived outside of school. I didn't know if she had a boyfriend, dated, or even liked guys. The Heckler knew a last-minute, awkward effort would further decrease my odds of success. I hadn't developed any type of friendship or rapport with Jackie. I barely knew her name; I'm sure she didn't know mine. Simply stated, my likelihood of success was somewhere between slim and none. Having almost no chance for success was just what the Heckler/Eddie wanted.

Hecklers can be devious. They encourage us to try and to then fail miserably. After a humiliating failure, it will be much easier to persuade me not to make similar attempts in the future. The possibilities of rejection, disappointment, failure, and humiliation will seem far too great.

Beaver Cleaver had a similar experience in the episode where Eddie convinced him to buy a high-priced accordion so he could become a rich and famous musician. It sounded reasonable at the time and set Beaver up for certain failure and big trouble with his parents. (Beaver bought the expensive instrument without his parents' knowledge nor consent.) The Heckler, in the same way, gave me the encouragement to go to that dorm room to almost certain failure and eventual humiliation.

This would be my last opportunity to see Jackie. In my mind she was the perfect match for me (The Heckler likes to intensify things). She was very cute, and what I considered my type: attractive, athletic, bright, outgoing, and full of life. I was terrified. The hope and fantasy of having Jackie as a girlfriend (with the Heckler's encouragement) carried me across campus, up the stairs, and down the long hall to her dorm room.

Unfortunately for me, she was there, and worse yet, so were her two roommates. You can't have a good humiliation without an audience. I softly knocked on the door. I waited for a moment, considered giving up and going home. The Heckler/Eddie told me to knock again, assuring me I would be successful. I knocked again, a little harder this time. Jackie opened the door. Despite her confused expression, she looked beautiful. I remember saying something like, "Since we will never see each other again, could we exchange phone numbers?" The next thing I remember was the door slamming and hearing all three girls laughing through the door.

I stood there, frozen...stunned...I'll never forget the room number 222 staring me in the face and hearing the three girls' unrestricted laughter ringing in my ears. All I could do was turn around and start slumping down that long hallway. I was hoping and praying they weren't watching me through the peephole in the door. I felt completely humiliated, embarrassed, and ashamed, just what the Heckler wanted. For the next thirty years, it was nearly impossible for me to ask a girl for a date.

The Heckler inhibits you from living your life to the fullest. The Heckler managed it so I couldn't ask a question, get in front of a group, or ask a girl for a date. It's almost impossible to achieve your dreams with so many self-imposed limitations. When you learn what the Heckler is up to, you can begin to transform like I have, from a zero to a hero.

> "A hero is an ordinary individual who finds the strength to persevere and endure in spite of overwhelming obstacles."
> ~Christopher Reeve

No More Excuses

My beautiful friend Susan knows in her heart she is worthy of a relationship. She is exceptionally intelligent with a sharp with and a cute figure. Yet, every time a responsible and pleasant man as much as approaches her, Susan comes up with immediate excuses (with the Heckler's assistance) why he isn't worth meeting.

Susan's Heckler says:

- He's got to be too religious.
- He is too tall, short, fat, skinny, smart, not-smart enough, not good-looking enough, too good-looking, or talks too little, or too much.
- He looks like he makes too little, or too much money.
- He might live too far away.
- He won't like me, so why consider him?
- His race or background will be a problem.

Susan's Heckler can go through that list in less than three seconds. Just about any man and, unfortunately, Susan never had a chance. In reality, it was Susan's Heckler, not her own intuition, intellect, or her heart doing the talking. Stop making excuses for not striving for your dreams. It's time to recognize the Heckler is behind it. It's time to no longer permit the Heckler to stymie your dreams.

Just Notice

You can start transforming the Heckler into your Hero by being aware. Notice anytime you are not working and moving toward your dreams and goals. This takes awareness, practice, and patience. It's extremely important to not berate or put yourself down for being tricked, forgetting, or blindsided by the Heckler's antics. Berating yourself is just another one of the Heckler's tricks to further trip you up.

Pay attention to what you are doing and not doing. Pretend you are watching yourself on a monitor. Pretend you are outside of yourself looking at and observing your activities. Are you being productive? Are your actions and behaviors matching your goals and dreams? Are you wasting time and energy on nonproductive activities? The trick is to slow down, to have the patience, awareness, and the discipline to notice. It seems easy, but the Heckler will do anything to keep you distracted.

Practice noticing. Make paying attention and awareness a habit. Make a mental note to stop and notice every quarter to half hour to how you are doing. If you miss a few half hours, it's perfectly normal. Start from right now to pay attention. Check yourself to see if you are engaged in dream-enhancive activities, or are you being distracted?

Being distracted is like a kind of fog. The Heckler, like Eddie Haskell, persuades you to do something, anything other than work toward your dreams. The distracting activity may sound reasonable. The activity may seem to be the best choice at the time. Checking emails, reading the paper, or calling a friend may seem to be a priority. The Heckler constantly convinces you into doing these unproductive activities. Consider if what you are doing, thinking, or feeling right now could be another method or tool in the Heckler's arsenal.

Please stop for a moment, even if you think you are on track. There is a good chance you are being motivated by the Heckler. Pause and ask yourself, am I doing what I had planned to do today? Is this activity in my highest interest? Is this the best thing I could be doing? Is this endeavor something the Heckler talked me into believing is important? If you are off track, don't berate yourself; simply shift to the activities you had planned.

When you notice the Heckler's tricks, after you adjust back to working toward your dreams and completed some focused work, it's extremely important for you to celebrate your victory over the Heckler. Treat yourself: Call or visit a friend. Go out for lunch or dinner. Take in a movie. Watch your favorite television show. Read a book. Be proud of yourself. You have taken a major step toward having the life you love and living your dreams.

Dream Notes

To Jump-Start Your Dreams

Don't take things personal...
People often mistake a no as a personal rejection.

STOP IT!

The Heckler's Favorite Rants

One of my dreams is to perform stand-up comedy. My friend Jay whom I had met at an improv class invited me to a comedy workshop which meets every Monday night. Jay said I could go and just watch. He told me the instructor could help me come up with some ideas for jokes. I remembered my friend Ellen telling me, "That's how I came up with material for my routine." In the list below you can see how things worked out for me regarding my dream of performing stand-up comedy.

Here is a week-by-week description of what happened and the technique, or rant, that the Heckler used to block my dream.

Week 1. The voice in my head (the Heckler) reminded me I don't have material. I decided to wait and go the next week, when I'm fully prepared.

Modifies: There was no RULE I had to have material.

Week 2. I had some good ideas, but I didn't take the time to write them down.

Procrastination: The Heckler tricked me into not writing down my ideas. I had magically forgotten, ha-ha. The Heckler was stronger than my desire. Without my ideas on paper, I could look foolish. I might be humiliated for my lack of preparation. It seems that no matter what, I'm going to be embarrassed. I stayed home that night and watched reruns of *Mash.* Not showing up created more shame and embarrassment, shame and embarrassment that the Heckler used against me to stifle my dream.

Week 3. I couldn't find my notes. I couldn't go without any notes, and the more I looked, the more frustrated I got.

Unorganized/Frustration: The Heckler made sure I misplaced my notebook. Not being able to find it, I became increasingly frustrated. By the time I found it, I was so upset that being funny seemed impossible.

Week 4. It was a really beautiful day, and I decided to watch the sunset. It was a tough decision, but the voice (the Heckler) told me I would receive inspiration by the beautiful sunset.

Distraction: The Heckler makes sure we notice everything but what we should be focused on. Without knowing it is your Heckler, you often choose nonproductive activities. Note: There were six other sunsets since I missed the last class. The Heckler chose just the sunset on Monday to admire.

Week 5. The material wasn't perfect. I didn't practice enough. I must be the best. Anything other than the best in the class is not acceptable.

Perfectionism: We live in an imperfect world. We all make mistakes, especially the first few times. The Heckler convinced me I must do it perfectly the first time or not at all.

Week 6. I just didn't feel good and might even be sick.

Sick and/or Tired: The Heckler convinces you that you are either too sick, too tired, or both.

Week 7. I had planned on going, but I completely forgot. Just as well because I also forgot to work on the material…again.

Amnesia: The Heckler easily makes you completely forget about your projects, goals, and dreams.

Week 8. I spent about ten hours working on my opening and conclusion. I forgot all about the assignment to write three short jokes. The Heckler makes things much more difficult than they need to be and changes the work. Focusing only on my opening and introduction, I didn't get around to, or even think about the assignment.

Intensifies and Complicates: The Heckler makes the job much larger than necessary and excessively complicated. Most tasks are left incomplete. You exert so much effort you are unable to do anything else. Often you overlook the most important aspects.

Week 9. The Heckler stated, "Ellen and Jay and all the rest of the students are so much better. I'm not good enough. I don't deserve to do stand-up comedy. I'll just forget the whole thing."

Comparing and Analyzing: The Heckler will always convince you, you aren't good or worthy enough. They persuade you to give up and quit.

Week 10. My dogs need walking, I haven't called my mother in a month, and the Angels are playing the Red Sox. The Heckler convinced me, that wasn't a good night for comedy.

> **Priorities:** You can start asking yourself: Is this the most important thing I could be doing right now? Determine who is making this decision, you or the Heckler.

Week 11. This week I had so many different things to do. The laundry needed to be done. I was behind at work. The dogs needed baths. The kitchen looked like a health hazard. There is so much to do, I felt overwhelmed. I ended up watching movies all night.

> **Overwhelm:** I went into overload and did nothing. Just what the Heckler wanted. Do you believe that was my best self doing the talking?

Week 12. My God, this was a twelve-week class and I missed the first eleven! Why go to the last one? This class would have been fun. I could have learned a lot. I would have met interesting people. I could have worked toward one of my dreams. I'm so FRUSTRATED with myself. Why do I mess everything up? I'm a no-good loser.

> **Low self-esteem:** The Heckler takes advantage of where you feel less-than to easily control, shame, and convinces you to quit.

The Heckler heckles you to prevent you from making mistakes. They protect you from fear, embarrassment, shame, and any possibility of failure. Anytime you aren't working toward your dreams, stop and ask yourself who is doing the talking? Who is making the decisions? Is it you or the Heckler? Chances are it's not your higher self talking!

Pay attention to what you just did, said, or thought. Does it look like something on the list from the twelve weeks above? Look at the Heckler's rants, behaviors, and directives in appendix #3. These are all behaviors my Heckler got me to do for decades. Can you match your behavior, activity, or excuse with one from the list or from the twelve weeks?

> "A dreamer is one who can only find his way by moonlight, and his punishment is that he sees the dawn before the rest of the world."
> ~Oscar Wilde

Tell the Heckler No

Start to say no by slowing down. Notice when you are not moving toward your dreams. Say to yourself, (and it's okay to talk to yourself), "Something is wrong." Talking to yourself will interrupt the Heckler. Match what you have noticed with a rant, behavior, or saying from the appendix #3. By completing this exercise you will be well on your way to transforming the Heckler into your Hero. Simply tell the Heckler, "No." Announce, "I'm no longer falling for that trick. I believe in my dreams and my life more than your heckling. Thank you, I no longer need your help!"

The Heckler can be understood as your own inner parents. The protective parents you had as an infant, before you developed the skills to defend and take of yourself. As a child, you were constantly bombarded with commands, warnings, and orders. Mostly you heard the words: "No," "Don't," and "You Can't."

Here are a few more examples:

- Be seen and not heard.
- Do it my way.
- Don't ask any more questions.
- Don't blame your mother.
- Don't cross the street.
- Don't cry.
- Don't do anything without my permission.
- Don't do this, don't do that, or the other thing.
- Don't look at me that way.
- Don't rock the boat.
- Don't say, or do that.
- Don't talk back to me.
- Don't talk to strangers.
- Don't think that.
- Don't touch that.
- Don't try anything new, untried, different, or strange.
- Don't try to cook by yourself.
- Don't wear that.
- Only cross the street with an adult.
- Only do what I tell you.
- You can't fight city hall.

You can easy add many more of your own. It's a wonder you ever did, or do anything! The problem is that you still listen to the Heckler,   just like the Heckler was your real parent and you were an adolescent child. Heckling was intended to protect you. Heckling is no longer useful as you are now an adult. You can now recognize it for what it is and simply say, "NO."

Few had perfect parents. Most parents did the best they could. They had no idea their looking after your safety could cripple your growth. Most parents don't realize the benefits of allowing you to fail, try new things, and do things on your own. They never imagined you would develop and carry an inner critic into your adulthood.

Just like your parents, you do the best you can with what you know and how you were brought up. You developed your own Heckler to guard yourself from potential, or perceived danger. It's a carryover from our caveman/women ancestors and the perilous life they lead. If they didn't have a healthy set of fears (the Heckler) to keep them safe, they would be living a very short life.

It's your responsibility to parent yourself. You can now disregard the Heckler's rants, behaviors, and sayings. You can transform the heckles into signs and signals to guide your progress. You can see the heckles as information pointing out the areas that simply require more attention. With better information you can be prepared to take more risks, try new things, and meet new people. You no longer need to put your growth, development, and unfoldment on hold.

Now that you understand the Heckler's purpose, it is much easier to detect it. You have removed the veil of secrecy from the Heckler. With the Heckler in plain sight, you can TELL THE HECKLER NO.

"High achievers spot rich opportunities swiftly, make big decisions quickly, and move into action immediately. Follow these principles and you can make your dreams come true."
~Robert H. Schuller

Become a Warrior

Becoming a warrior has been a challenging and an important step for me in transforming my Heckler. You need to do more than just be aware of the Heckler. You need to learn and memorize his or her behaviors, rants, and sayings. Anything keeping you from moving closer to your goals and dreams needs to be transformed. You need to be absolutely determined to transform what is not acceptable in your life.

To be a warrior has not been an easy matter for me. I was taught compassion, understanding, helping, service, and nonviolence are the holiest of virtues. My parents taught me to avoid any and all types of conflict and confrontation. I was taught not to stand up for myself. In our family, considering ourselves first was not the correct way to be.

Some of the factors that contributed to my way of thinking were:

- A concern of hurting or offending someone
- Concern of not being liked
- Concern that I wasn't good enough
- Fear of confrontation
- Fear that someone might be displeased with me
- Feelings of shame
- Inability to stand up for myself
- Low self-esteem
- Need to not make anyone angry

My parents taught me to always be kind and to never hurt or confront anyone. No wonder I had so much trouble with the Heckler. I was paralyzed. I was unable to do anything that could possibly hurt, upset, or irritate anyone, including the Heckler! The Heckler literally controlled my life.

The keys to my recovery were surprisingly simple. I realized that I took my need to be kind too literally. We all have similar internal struggles, wars, and conflicts. Joseph Campbell in his book *"The Hero's Journey,"* pointed out we all have trials to confront,   trials as part of a journey that everyone must take to achieve their dreams. We all must take our own hero's journey, a journey that involves conflict and confrontation. Now that you know you have your own hero's journey, you know a major part of your journey is to transform your Heckler into your Hero. It is a required journey and one of the most important journeys you will ever take.

Conclusion

Transforming the Heckler into your Hero is the most important thing you can do in catching your dreams. Your inner Heckler is a kind of inner parent, a parent who, like most all parents, has your best interests at heart. Parents want to protect their children. Your Heckler, just like a parent, wants to keep you safe.

Your Heckler starts when you are very young. Remember the times when you were most embarrassed, put down, or laughed at? These are the times the Heckler uses to keep you down, to keep you safe. The Heckler's job is to make sure you don't get embarrassed, put down, or laughed at again. The best method to make sure you are not put into that situation again is to distract you into doing other activities like eating ice cream, watching TV, playing video games, or sleeping, all activities that do not lead you to living the life of your dreams.

Now that you are an adult, now that you can cross the street by yourself, you can be aware of the Heckler, thank the Heckler, and move forward toward your goals and dreams. You now have a list to be aware of the Heckler's rants, distractions, and agenda. You realize that the Heckler works in stealth, in secrecy to avoid detection. You have the tools to realize who is determining your actions, actions that can be nothing but a distraction or can be dream-enhancing.

Congratulations! By transforming the Heckler into your Hero, you are well on your way to catching your dreams and living the life you were born to live.

DREAMS
COME
TRUE

Recap — Transform the Heckler Into Your Hero

On a Mission-Not from God: your Heckler wants to keep you safe by keeping your life small.

The Voice: the inner negative voice that isn't you.

I See You: awareness of the Heckler is your first step toward freedom.

The Heckler-Your Inner Critic: don't allow the inner critic to control you.

The Heckler's Stealth Mode: the Heckler is often unnoticed.

The Shame, Blame, Guilt Game: the Heckler persuades you to dwell on your self-critical nature.

Our Childhood Stories: we often use our childhood stories as an excuse to keep us from our dreams.

Hecklers Create Failure: a reason or excuse not to move forward.

No More Excuses: stop it.

Just Notice: pay attention to how the Heckler is trying to manipulate you.

The Heckler's Favorite Rants: when you are aware of the Heckler's rants, you are no longer controlled by them.

Tell the Heckler No: interrupt the Heckler by saying "No."

Become a Warrior: be determined to transform what is not acceptable in your life.

Handwritten note:
① Dream Big
② Set goal
③ Take Action

Dreamtime
Do Try This at Home

1. Remember the Heckler is out there. In other words, be on the lookout and notice when you are not feeling empowered, are inclined to procrastinate or get distracted. See if you can name the distraction, behavior, or rant. Make a copy of the appendix page #3, the Heckler's rants. Carry it with you. Post it on the bathroom mirror and on your fridge. Spend this week and do your best to notice every hour what the Heckler is up to. Are you doing the most important task? Are you doing what you planned? Does it lead you toward your goals and dreams? If you are not moving toward your goals and dreams, check the list, and name how you were Heckled.

2. Take a few minutes and write about a time in your childhood when you were embarrassed, put down, or laughed at. Write about how this incident(s) kept you from moving toward your dreams, how the incident kept you from living a larger life. Write in detail what areas of your life you have avoided. For example,

public speaking, an intimate relationship, moving, a project, hobby, or changing to a job you love.

3. **Make a Commitment**

Choose just one thing you are going to do within the next forty-eight hours that will move you toward your goals and dreams. Write it down as a contract.

I _____ commit to
Name

_____ to be
Doing this one task

completed by _____   _____
Date   Signature

4. After you have completed the task, write in your journal how it made you feel.

5. **Have Fun**

It is imperative that you reward yourself for doing a good job! A good day doesn't mean perfection. It means consistency, dailiness, and awareness. At the end of a good day, give yourself a reward. Take in a dinner, movie, read a book, call a friend, and/or go out for coffee. For me, I enjoy going to yoga, and I'm on the way there as I finish this. Go have some fun; you deserve it.

Declaration: I no longer fear, hate, ignore, or run from the Heckler. I simply see the heckling as an alert to the direction I need to go. I'm empowered to transform the Heckler into my Hero.

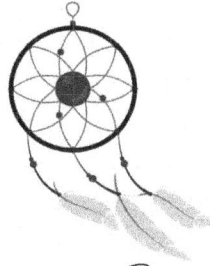

Your
DREAM CATCHER

Chapter V. Love Your Body

"Love the skin you're in."

~Dove commercial

Loving your body is very essential to every aspect of living your dreams.   You have to use your body to discover, live, and manifest your dreams. Loving your body is, in reality, also loving yourself and your dreams.

Take in a long, slow, deep breath. Slowing and deepening your breath helps you to be more relaxed. With practice you can lower your heart rate by controlling your breath. When you are aware of your breathing and slow it down, you will be more clear-minded. A clear mind helps you with clarity to determine and then manifest your dreams.

Awareness of breath gives you a connection to yourself and a bridge between you and your body. In the past I tended to stay busy. I didn't take the time to slow down to think, to actually contemplate my dreams. Awareness of breathing is a step that gives you that time to give your dreams the necessary attention they deserve.

Catch your dreams

Love

* strong affection for another arising out of kinship or personal ties

* warm attachment, enthusiasm, or devotion

* the object of attachment, devotion, or admiration

*unselfish loyal and benevolent

Merriam-Webster

Enjoy a Nap

It is very important to enjoy a nap. A nap is one of the greatest things you can do for our body. A nap is something that many rarely do. Most of us think we have to be busy doing something every single moment. Your body needs to regenerate, to recharge, and to feel refreshed. A nap makes a statement that you are important and loved. Your body is important; you cannot easily manifest your dreams without a healthy body. As mentioned above, loving your body is loving yourself and your dreams. Loving your dreams gives you purpose. Purpose gives you energy, energy to manifest and make your dreams real.

Taking a nap says that you are important. A nap also helps your body do more. When you take the time to take a nap, you get more done. What happens when we don't plug in the battery for an electric car? The car will eventually stop running.

A nap will also help your mind think more clearly. When you enjoy a nap for a few minutes, you gift your body, mind, and spirit with a chance to recharge, recreate, and regenerate. Without a clear head and strong body you can't effectively function. Below are some ideas that will help motivate you to take a nap.

* Your thoughts will be clearer and you will feel stronger.
* You will be more alert and more aware of what is going on.
* You will feel better.
* You will get more done.

Most importantly, you will be able to work towards your dreams more efficiently, effectively, and easily.

Start by declaring to you and your body: "*I am worth it, and my dreams are worth it.*"

Thank Your Body

You body is amazing, and you tend to take it for granted. You tend to take much of life for granted. It's a miracle that the sun comes up every day. What has nature done to create a bird and for it to sing? Your magnificent body only has to drink a little bit of water and eat a little bit of food (even junk food), and sleep a little, and it does almost anything you ask of it. If you decide you want to wiggle your finger, how many fibers, tendons, muscles, ligaments, and nerves have to coordinate to simply wiggle a finger?

Blood is circulating throughout your entire body. Blood is constantly replenishing, nourishing, and detoxing your body. Your body is an amazing miracle. Appreciate your body by noticing the value in your life. See the value in your dreams. Notice your body and all it does and say, "Thank you."

Your Body is Amazing

Think of your body as a separate organism. Many take better care of their car than their own body. You wash and detail your car. You give it the highest quality of gas, and change the oil every 3,000 miles. You would never stuff a hot dog, fries, and a diet coke into your car's gas tank and expect it to run all day and all night. Why do you do it to your body?

Slow down and notice the amazing gift of your body, this magnificent mechanism you get around in. You can begin to recognize and value of your body when you comprehend its true value. What would it cost to re-create it? (if it was possible) What would just a finger cost? How much would it be to buy a human liver, heart, or the most amazing computer, your brain? It could add up to over a trillion dollars.

Celebrate Your Body

Another way to honor your body is to sing, skip, laugh, and dance -- every day. Take the time to honor, respect, and celebrate your body. Gift your body with what it needs to be healthy and happy. Get up and move, take time to play, and create some endorphins in your system. You and your body will love it. Laugh out loud. Laughing will reduce stress and improve your immune system. Sing and you will feel uplifted, energized, and cheerful.

Jump and dance like you did as a child. Sing like no one is watching. Laugh like you don't have a care in the world. It is unfortunate in our society most were instructed to act like a grown-up. We were taught to not act childish. I recommend for your mental, physical, and emotional well-being, act, play, and laugh like a child.

Children are not afraid to dance, laugh, and sing. I remember years ago I was in Pasadena, California standing near Colorado Boulevard, there was a school bus across and down the street about a hundred yards away filled with third or fourth graders. There was so much noise, and because of all the ruckus going on inside, I thought for a brief moment that the bus was on fire. What I soon discovered was that the kids were just enjoying life. There was so much activity the bus was actually rocking back and forth. It was like it was New Year's Eve. Once I realized everything was okay, it was wonderful to witness. The more you can allow yourself to be free, the better your life will be. Allow yourself to sing, dance, laugh, and skip every day.

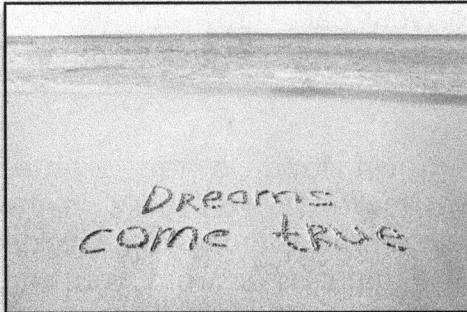

Organic

* forming an integral element of a whole

*having systematic coordination of parts

* having the characteristics of an organism

Merriam-Webster

Dreams come true

Eat Organic

It is important that you eat well. You can't eat Coco Puffs all day long and expect your body to run perfectly while working sixteen hours a day. Eat to live. Take time out and enjoy your food. When you eat, turn off the television and put your books, magazines, computer, and newspapers away. Eat in your dining room. Take your time and enjoy your meals. Focus on simply eating, enjoy the experience, and allow your body to fully assimilate the nutrients of the food.

Support your body so your body can support your dreams. Take the time to actually chew your food thoroughly. It will support your digestion system to work better. Have a strong intention that your meals will give you energy, vitality, and a spark of life to dive your toward your dreams.

Set the intention that your food will give you vitality and energy as you are preparing it, and even when you are shopping for it at the grocery store or the farmers market. Take time out and dine with friends and family. Treat yourself and go out once a week to a nice dinner. Go out with a friend, or go by yourself, and have a healthy, wholesome, organic meal. Eating healthy is a strong statement to yourself and the Universe, THAT YOU ARE WORTHY. Honor your body and yourself by eating well. Eating well is like investing in the best gas for your car. Throw out the Coco Puffs. Invest in the most important thing in the world, your body.

Good, organically grown food is the greatest investment that you can ever make. Do you really want to save a few pennies, but therefore have to ingest pesticides and dangerous hormones? If there is a word you can't pronounce on the label of the food, don't buy it. If it comes in a bag, a box, or a can, and isn't organic, don't buy it. As more of us start to eat what is good for us, the food prices will go down. Eat slowly and have the intent that the food you eat is supporting you and your dreams. You are worth it. Your dreams are worth it.

"Everything you need to know is within you. Listen. Feel. Trust the body's wisdom."
~Dan Millman

Move It

Shake it, dance, and move your body. Your body is like a race horse or a Ferrari race car; it's designed to be exercised. There is a reason there is an endorphin high when you move your body. The endorphin high is a way that your creator gave you to encourage you to exercise! You are going to receive this reward for moving your body. If you don't move it, your body will atrophy. If you don't work toward your dreams, your dreams will also atrophy.

There are so many easy things you can do to exercise your body. Instead of hoping and praying to get the closest parking space, park in a lousy parking space and walk. You don't have to buy a gym membership to exercise. You don't have to put on a gym outfit and drive to the gym. You can make exercise a part of your everyday life. You can vigorously vacuum, wash the car, and clean out the fridge. You can walk the dogs three or four times a day. Your dogs will love you! Take the stairs, dance, or hop up and down. Walk more briskly, or go for a run, jog, or better yet a hike. I love the convenience of running. All you have to do is go outside. There is no need to drive to a gym when you run.

Open your front door and start running. It's that quick and easy. Make exercise a priority. Make a plan to exercise as part of your day. Your exercise time is one of the most important things you can do for your dreams. Exercise is just as important as eating, and breathing. Put exercise on your calendar. Make moving it a priority.

Eliminate Clutter

Eliminate clutter sounds like it should be in another chapter or even another book. For me, eliminating clutter makes me more relaxed. When I'm relaxed, my body feels better. I start by eliminating clutter in my mind. I can eliminate the clutter in my mind by just doing nothing. You can call it meditating, sitting, or just taking it easy. I like the song "Don't Worry Be Happy". By being happy, I eliminate mind clutter. To eliminate mind clutter, I think less.

Take the clutter out of your rooms. Make your home less cluttered. When I clean everything off my desk, I feel better. When I feel better, my body feels better. Cleaning my home is a wonderful stress reducer. Eliminating house clutter helps me clear my mind and relaxes my body. Then I can move towards my goals and dreams more easily. Eliminating clutter does not stop at my desk and mind. Relationships that are not working need to kindly be eliminated. You don't have to be rude, just avoid relationships that aren't working.

Make life simpler. Eliminate clutter from your mind. Stop gossiping. Only speak about things that are supportive of your body and your dreams. Remove negative thinking. Don't say or think that things are hard or times are bad. Clear your mind and stay positive. Remove the negative self-talk. If your body feels less than perfect, say, "It's getting better." If you aren't living your dreams, say, "I'm getting closer every day." Eliminating clutter in your environment, mind, voice, and relationships makes room for your dreams.

Eliminating clutter makes room for your body to move better, feel better, and be better.

Dream Notes

To jump start your Dreams

Schedule your workout
or
play-outs first...

That's right put it in your calendar...NOW!

Dress for Your Dreams

Another thing you can do to demonstrate value for yourself and your body is pay attention to how you dress. Go all out. You, your body, and your dreams are worth it. When you dress up, you are saying to your body, "I look good. I'm beautiful. I have value, and so do my dreams!" In reality, your body is worth several trillion dollars. Really. If science was to attempt to duplicate this amazing apparatus known as your body, it would take trillions of dollars, and the scientists and engineers wouldn't come close to replicating you. One could never replace your body with all the money in the world.

When you dress up, it makes you feel better. It demonstrates respect and honor. This respect and honor then transforms into all areas of your life, including your dreams.

Dressing up expresses an attitude of success, a success that may not as yet be materialized. It's like the expression, *fake it 'til you make it*. Dress like you would when you have achieved and are living your dreams. When you start looking like you are one of the highest-paid speakers in the world, you are more likely to be a well-compensated speaker. You can make dressing for your dreams an everyday experience. Even when going to the market, you can dress neatly, cleanly, and sharply. Make sure your clothing is clean and pressed. You will feel as if your dreams have already been achieved.

I started throwing out my older clothes. I no longer wear the old stuff. In the past, I would wear my old stuff because I was saving the newer, better clothing for the future. I would wear the older clothes because I didn't want to mess up the new ones. Now I only wear my best whether it is my best casual or my Sunday best. I'm telling my body and my dreams that I'm worth it.

"I sing the body electric."
~Walt Whitman

Tune In

It is extremely important to stay tuned in and interested in your dreams. This is something that has been a challenge for me. A great method to stay tuned in is through information. Now that we have the Internet and search engines, we can be informed about anything regarding our body. I understand that if you line up the DNA in your body that it would reach around the moon and back. To find out how to honor your body, simply Google it. You can learn what foods are best for you. You can buy, read, and study books on how to exercise and love your body. You can talk to friends. There is an infinite amount to learn in support of your body. Tune in and your body will be better-equipped to support your dreams.

Hire a Trainer

You can hire a personal trainer to stay motivated and to provide you with accountability. A trainer will also teach you and give you an individualized routine to follow. Most trainers can help you with a nutrition and diet plan. It is important to be interested in exercising your body. When you are interested, it's like interest in the bank. You can earn a return, or interest on what you put in your bank account. You will earn interest or receive a return when you put effort into your body. You will get a percentage back with huge dividends. The major dividend is a body that is capable of moving toward your dreams.

Pamper Your Body

It's important that you pamper your body. At least twice a month, get a massage. Your body is worth it. Your body needs that caring. It needs to get the kinks out. Go on a run at the beach. Take your dog for a walk. Take yoga classes. Nurture yourself by getting a manicure and/or a pedicure. Take a bubble bath or go into a Jacuzzi. Go for a hike in nature.

Do nothing. That small break will be extremely beneficial for your body. It is imperative for your dreams for you to love your body. Your amazing machine called your body needs respect, love, and care. Give thanks and appreciate your body more often, so you can do more in the world.

Conclusion

If you are serious about catching your dreams, taking care of your body is a top priority. You simply can't get from point A to point B without a means to get there. If you don't feel well, if you can't move, or it's difficult, then your odds of realizing and catching your dreams are greatly diminished.

I'm speaking from experience. I suffered from chronic exhaustion for over twenty-five years. Prior to the illness, I was able to achieve anything I set my mind to. During the twenty-five years of fatigue, as Dr. Phil would ask, "How is that working for you?" and my answer was always, "Not so well." Having a body that didn't function properly didn't allow me to move efficiently toward my dreams.

Taking care of your body is taking care of yourself and your dreams. Now that I no longer have the fatigue, I have the energy and motivation to work/play for and toward my dreams. The fact I'm writing and finishing this chapter is living proof. For all those years, writing was work, difficult, and tiring. Now that I've taken care and loved my body back to health, writing this book is fun and exciting.

Start from wherever you are and follow the ideas and topics in this chapter to eat a healthy diet, exercise, rest, and love your body. Realize that when you are energized and feeling great, you will have the motivation and ability to catch and realize your dreams. You will be able to appreciate the gift of having a body in which to move and manifest your dreams. You will be a Dream Catcher.

DREAMS COME TRUE

Recap — Love Your Body

Enjoy a Nap: it's important to regenerate, recharge, and refresh your body.

Thank Your Body: notice the value of and appreciate all your body can do.

Your Body is Amazing: take note of the incredible gift of your body.

Celebrate Your Body: sing, dance, and skip like you did as a child.

Eat organic: support your body, so your body can support your dreams.

Move it: if you don't exercise, your body and your dreams atrophy.

Eliminate Clutter: you will have more space to create your dreams.

Dress for Your Dreams: go all out; you and your dreams are worth it.

Tune In: stay interested in your dreams.

Hire a Trainer: a trainer will help you stay motivated and give you accountability.

Pamper your Body: take care of yourself, so you can take care of your dreams.

Dreamtime
Do Try This at Home

1. By the end of next week—get a message. Write about how loving your body has already supported your dreams.

2. Take a walk in nature before Sunday night. Be peaceful and calm
while you walk, pay attention to your body and allow yourself to sense what your body and dreams need next.

3. Dance, skip, and shake your body. When you have some privacy, turn on your favorite music extra loud and dance to it. Shake things up and have some fun. Act childlike, dance as crazily and silly as you can. Remember, no one is watching. Dance as if you don't have a care in the world. Journal about how it felt. Are you more positive? Does it bring anything new for your dreams?

4. Give yourself time to rest. Take a nap. While you are resting, listen to your body for what it needs more of

(it could be more rest).   Whatever it is, within forty-eight hours, give it to your body.

Declaration: From this day onward I will honor, respect, and nurture my body.

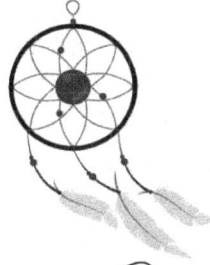

Your
DREAM CATCHER

Chapter VI. Learn to Succeed

"Success truly is the result of good judgment. Good judgment is the result of experience, and experience is often the result of bad judgment."

~Anthony Robbins

You already know how to succeed. The proper statement is that you simply need to relearn how to succeed. Deep down in your heart you already have the answers inside. When you relearn how to succeed you will emerge as the person you truly are inside. This book and this chapter will help you with your transformation.

To begin, you must know what you want to succeed at. Do you want to succeed at love, life, fame, or fortune? One of the most successful persons ever is Coach John Wooden of UCLA. Coach Wooden said, "Success is peace of mind which is the direct result of self-satisfaction and knowing you did your best you were capable of becoming." There is no measuring nor competition involved. Simply be the best you that you already are.

Catch your dreams

Learn

* to gain knowledge or understanding of or skill in by study, instruction, or experience

* to come to be able

* to come to realize

Do What You Love

The first step in revealing the real you is uncovering your passion and purpose. You don't have to save the world. You don't have to be Froto in *The Lord of the Rings*. You can simply do what you love. Match your skills and experience with what you love. It will be helpful for you to try the exercises at the end of this chapter. Your passion should be something fun and exciting for you. What do you love? What is fun for you? What would you do for free? Are your passions and dreams exciting, hopeful, and inspiring? Does your purpose serve you and others? Are you currently serving yourself and the world?

Robert H. Schuller stated, "What would you do if you couldn't fail?" If you go by Schuller's statement, you will easily uncover your purpose. Joseph Campbell advised you to, "Follow your bliss." I say, "Do what you love, and have fun." Move your mental and emotional blocks and obstacles out of the way. One of the obstacles is to realize and know that it's okay and good to do what you love! Society often tells you that it is not okay to have fun while at work. You are not supposed to enjoy work. Work is supposed to be difficult and uncomfortable. The concept that work must make you suffer is a fallacy. It's okay to do what you love. In fact, it is mandated by Spirit, the Universe, or God for you to do what you love. Let go of any thought patterns and all misguided beliefs that it's not okay to enjoy yourself.

"I am always doing that
which I cannot do,
in order that I may learn
how to do it."
~ Pablo Picasso

Make Enough Mistakes

Making mistakes could be more difficult for some than others. You may not be comfortable in making mistakes. In John Holt's book, *How Children Learn*, John wrote, "Children love the world, and that is why they are so good at learning about it." It is logical that if you love what you do, you will learn more easily. You will easily live your dreams and follow your bliss.

When you love and then live your dreams, you will easily learn the additional steps to do whatever is necessary. All you need to do is take the next step. The next step doesn't have to be perfect. You just need to take it. Michael Beckwith, the founder of the Agape International Spiritual

Center, taught about tripping when he said, "When you trip, you trip forward." Darren Lacroix, the 1999 world champion of public speaking in his championship speech said, "When you fall forward, you still make progress." It's perfectly fine to not know everything about whatever you are doing. Take that next step; even if you stumble, you stumble forward. When you trip and fall, that fall is guiding and preparing you for your next step toward your dreams. Your success in reaching your dreams is a matter of making enough mistakes. The more mistakes you make, the faster you will reach your dreams.

Check Your Attitude

Another thing that is very important to living your purpose is self-love. Nothing is more important than loving yourself. What goes with self-love is realizing your self-worth. You must realize that you are completely and totally invaluable, indispensable, and awesomely amazing. You could take all the computers in the word and they can't do what your brain can. Put the truth about yourself in perspective. Check your attitude. You are irreplaceable. You are incredibly and indispensably perfect. You make a difference in the world. The world would be in a far different place without you.

Rev. Michael Beckwith states, "God wants you to be successful." God didn't put you here to watch television. There is more to life than that. That is why it's imperative to have a positive, realistic attitude concerning your brilliance, so you can get up and make a difference in the world.

You need to have an attitude of gratitude for everything and everyone in your life, for yourself and for your dreams. Realize that having an attitude of gratitude will assist you in realizing your dreams. Having an attitude of gratitude makes life easier.

The Chinese have a word that translates to both the words obstacle and opportunity. This is because an obstacle, a problem, or a difficulty has the potential to bring forth something new, something that would not otherwise exist. Be grateful for any and all obstacles that come before you because you know it will bring you an opportunity. What is blocking you from your dreams is also a blessing to help you learn and grow.

"Once you learn to quit, it becomes a habit."
~Vince Lombardi

Create New Habits

Learning to succeed requires you to create new habits. One of the methods to create new habits is to cover the basis. You can begin to create new habits by knowing your purpose and then determining a set of goals to help you live your purpose. Another important step you must take is to dream. As a child, you may have gotten in trouble for dreaming or daydreaming. I recommend you daydream often. Dream of having fun and being excited. Dream of taking risks. Dream of being fearless.

Creativity comes from having a dream, and dreams are where real wisdom and inventiveness originate. As you dream and begin to notice your intuition and creativity, you realize that dreaming really is the building block of creativity. Once you pay attention to your synchronicity and the aha moments, you will be aware how important dreaming is to your life. In the book and movie *The Secret,* it is shown that when you expect to succeed, something magical happens. When you move into that space, you move into the magic of the universe and your dreams. As Jesus taught, "It is done to you as you believe." Trust just how important dreaming is to your creativity and how important creativity is to your success.

Dream Notes
To Jump-Start Your Dreams
Do one thing that you don't want to do to move you toward your Dreams.
TODAY!

Learn From Experts

You can learn from others by studying the greatest people in your field. If you want to be a basketball coach, learn everything you can about John Wooden. If you want to learn about inventiveness, study Steve Jobs. If you want to be an ice skater, model Kristi Yamaguchi. There is no rule that you have to reinvent the wheel. There is no law that states you have to be totally original. I really love something that my late brother Dan used to do when he supervised a sheltered workshop for special needs individuals. Whenever he was in a new town, he would look up where there was another sheltered workshop and take a tour. He learned some of their best ideas and took them back to his sheltered workshop. He would learn how they did things, what projects they chose, and how they operated. He would take one or two good ideas from every sheltered workshop he visited. It was no wonder he won so many awards for efficiency and placement of clients.

You can learn by modeling others. I was never great at shooting a basketball. What I would do to improve my shooting was pretend that I was Michael Jordan. I modeled his form and style. The results were amazing. When I shot the basketball as myself, I would make about two in ten three-point shots. When I pretended I was Michael, I would make five in ten shots. I was better because of two reasons: One, Michael had better form and technique; two, when I shot the ball as if I was Michael Jordan, I was more confident and expected the ball to go in.

Become a Next-Pert

When you are an expert, it's just natural to get things done. A friend of mine named Linda just gets things done. She jumps right into a project and moves. She is courageous and has no problem getting started and finishing a project or task. Linda manages a very large company with almost a hundred employees. She just jumps in and does whatever it takes to complete the task at hand. Linda makes it look easy because she is a next-pert.

You can start by just doing one thing. My good friend Mary calls it OTAD (One thing a day). If you do one thing every day, that would be 365 tasks completed in a year. That's 365 steps towards living your dreams. Dick Canfield, the co-author of the *Chicken Soup for the Soul* series, talked about improvement. He teaches that if you just improve yourself 2% a month, even without compounding, that's a 24% improvement in only a year, an improvement that has you moving toward your dreams. You can apply this technique to any or all of your dreams. I want to be 2% happier every month. In just four years I'll be twice as happy. There is a law that states, once a body is in motion it tends to stay in motion. Once you start and become a next-pert, it's much easier to transform your dreams into reality.

Work Your Plan with Persistence

Another thing that is important about learning to succeed and living your dreams is preparation. Jim, who was a valedictorian at the University of Riverside, credited being prepared as his biggest asset for his success. He said, "I cleared my desk space and made an appointment for myself to study." Jim also cleared the clutter out of his mind. He was focused, with a persistent plan to achieve his dreams.

My former boss Jose talked about scheduling your time to get motivated and be productive. His technique was to schedule lots of vacations and days off. His thinking was when you have a deadline, you will get more done. Jose was brilliant to have the deadline of going on vacation. Making the deadline of something good provided "the future thinking of our vacation to our present thinking of completing our work." With this plan and the persistence of wanting to be ready for our vacation, we achieved much more than we would have without Jose's motivational idea. You can also apply Jose's plan to learn to succeed and live the life of your dreams.

"The beautiful thing about learning is nobody can take it away from you."
~B.B. King

Conclusion

There is definitely an art to success. It is like the quote by Anthony Robbins at the beginning of this chapter, "Success truly is the result of good judgment. Good judgment is the result of experience, and experience is often the result of bad judgment." In other words, we learn to succeed. It isn't something that we are naturally born with. And the good news is, this chapter taught you the basics for success, so you can be a successful Dream Catcher.

It all starts with doing what you love. When you are doing what you love, it makes all the steps easy. You won't mind making enough mistakes. Having a positive attitude will be automatic, and creating new habits in doing what you love will be exactly what you want to do. When you are doing what you love and pursuing your dreams, you consult with experts without thinking. You make sure to consistently do at least one thing each day to move you closer to your dreams. You can't wait to learn what the next thing to do is in order to catch and live your dreams.

DREAMS
COME
TRUE

Recap — Learn to Succeed

Do What You Love: when you do what you love, it is easy and natural to succeed.

Make Enough Mistakes: the more mistakes you make, the faster you will reach your dreams.

Check Your Attitude: attitude equates to aptitude.

Create New Habits: learning to succeed requires you to create new habits.

Learn From Experts: you can learn from others by studying the greatest people in your field.

Become a Next-Pert: become an expert at doing what's next.

Work Your Plan with Persistence: have a persistent plan
to achieve your dreams.

Dreamtime
Do Try This at Home

1. Research your dreams. Learn from those who have done it before. Google it, read a book, check it out at your local library. Study how it has been done. For example, Michelle can read and study about how someone started a franchise. Jeremy can find a few articles from adults like himself who have completed their GED. And, I can interview three women who have magnificent husbands. Enjoy your discoveries by a week from tonight.

2. Prepare yourself to learn. Make your research area extra tidy and comfortable, with plenty of light. Make sure it's immaculately clean and inviting. Have fun doing it by the end of the week.

3. Do at least one thing to move closer to your dreams. Do at least one thing every day this week (OTAD). Do one thing even if it's just one phone call, one prayer, one affirmation, one dance step, one line of a poem, or one-page read. Start today.

4. Make a copy of the steps necessary to achieve your top dream. Put it by your bed and read it out loud every night before you go to sleep and every morning after waking up. Do this for at least the next twenty-one days.

Declaration: As of today, I will be patient with myself, and I will practice the steps necessary to learn how to achieve my dreams.

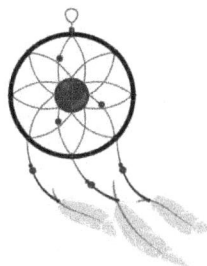

Your

DREAM CATCHER

Chapter VII. Tend to Your Dreams Daily

"Neither snow, nor rain, nor heat, nor gloom of night."

~ U.S. Postal Service

The reason I chose the quote above is because it shows dailiness. The quote communicates the determination and the priorities necessary to achieve your dreams. You will be required to tend to your dreams like the United States Postal Service, and their motto, "*Neither snow, nor rain, nor heat, nor gloom of night.* The Postal Service is dedicated to delivering the mail, **no matter what**. This is exactly the same way you should tend to your dreams.

I have made tending to my dreams a daily habit and practice. Make tending to your dreams a daily practice. Make it such a habit, it is something you do without thinking. You brush your teeth every day. You take a shower every day.

Why not tend to your dreams every day? Make working toward your dreams something you do first thing in the morning. Remember, tending to your dreams is not a chore. It's something that you love. Make tending to your dreams something you nurture and care for, just like you would your own child.

Make Time and Space for Your Dreams

Make time and space for your dreams. If your dreams are your number-one priority, you will naturally have time and a space for it. You can start to create space by cleaning the clutter in your work space. Your work space can be a desk, a work bench, or a place to study. Clean up the desktop of your computer. Make wherever you work an inviting place to be. Make it beautiful. Create a work/play space where you will be more inclined to enjoy working/playing.

You work/play space isn't limited to a physical space. It can be what's on your mind. Clear your mind of the past, and stop thinking about the future. Clear your mind. Come from an empty place of nothing so you can focus on your dreams. Your past is the past, and honestly, worrying about the future isn't productive. Stay focused on the present so you can move forward. Make a space for your dreams physically and mentally.

You can make an altar as a place to celebrate your dreams. You can have a picture board, a bulletin board, or a chalkboard where you can see representations of your dreams. Display items such as certificates, trophies, paychecks, and diplomas that show off your achievements. Catching your dreams is not just about achieving your dreams; it's also about your journey. When you are actively moving toward your dreams, you are, in a sense, already living them.

Put the activities that move you toward your dreams on your calendar. Putting your dream-achieving activities on your calendar is living proof that you are progressing toward a life that matters, a life with purpose, and a life with meaning. You have real evidence that you are moving toward the life you were born to live.

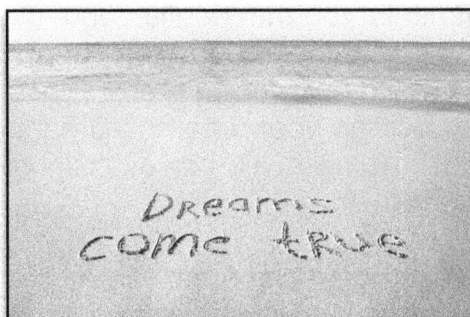

Tend

* Regularly or frequently behave in a particular way

* Care for or look after

* Give ones attention to

Merriam-Webster

You can create a storyboard (see appendix #2). I took the storyboard idea one step farther. I dedicated a wall in my office to my dream of writing this book. I created a detailed outline for this book. It included all the chapter titles, seven to twelve subjects for each chapter, plus quotes for each chapter. This wall made my dream real. I could actually see it. All that was left for me to do was fill in the blanks. You can do the same for the steps you have determined are essential to reach your dreams.

My coach, Rev. Joanne, teaches to work on your dreams first thing in the morning. She had me prepare my work space the night before. I cleared my work space and had whatever chapter I was working on already open in my computer and ready to write. This way everything was ready for me the moment I woke up. Reverend Joanne says, "Get it done before life gets in the way." When you work on your dreams first thing in the morning you'll get it done. Make it the most important task for the day, every day. When it is a habit, you won't have to think about it anymore. Doing your most important task first guarantees it gets done. My goal for you is to make your dreams and working toward them something you are thinking about all the time. Living and loving your dreams, working on them first thing every morning, will soon become a part of your daily activities.

Make an appointment for yourself to work on your dreams. You make appointments for the dentist and the doctor. You make appointments with friends and to take and attend classes. You make appointments for so many things, why not make appointments for living your dreams? Dreams are the most important thing in our life. I'll bet even more important than the dentist, ha-ha!

For me, I know it was my own Saboteur or Heckler who prevented me from working toward my dreams. I didn't make it a priority. I never set an appointment. When you start to make the most important things in your life (your dreams) a priority, you can build that priority into a habit. It is known that it takes twenty-one days to build a habit, so once you make that appointment for twenty-one days, working on and toward your dreams will become natural.

What is most important in your life? Why are you here? In my opinion, it is for you to create, to express, and be fully yourself. Creating and creativity is what you were born to do. You were born to live an outstanding life, to be happy, and to share your gifts and talents. There is nothing more important than to build the habit to create. Fall in love with yourself and your dreams. Start today and make a first-thing-in-the-morning appointment with your dreams.

Dream Breakdown Structure

You can also create a dream breakdown structure. A dream breakdown structure is like a set of blueprints for your project. The unique aspect is that you start at the end and work your way to where you are today.

For instance, if your dream is to write a book, your dream breakdown structure could start with you buying your book at Barnes & Noble, or ordering it on Amazon and receiving it via UPS. You work backwards from there. For example, the next step would be to approve the final version of your formatted book and cover design, then the formatting process. (Books need to be formatted for both a physical and ebook version) Getting your book edited and having the cover and back cover designed would be the next steps, then the rewriting process, the first draft, the outline, and lastly, the idea or concept. This style of dream breakdown structure is extremely effective. What makes the dream breakdown structure most effective is including dates for each stage to be completed. The Dream Breakdown Structure with completion dates is an extremely efficient method to assist you in catching your dreams

"Dreams or illusions, call them what you will, they lift us from the commonplace of life to better things."

~Henry Wadsworth Longfellow

Ask Your Dreams What They Want and What They Require

Your dreams have a life of their own. Take the time to ask them what they want and require. You often don't take the time to consider the most important thing in your life, your dreams. You think you are too busy. I used to use busyness to hide from what was most important to me. I was afraid of my big, crazy, wonderful dreams. Staying busy was a way of avoiding living my best life. Maryanne Williamson said it wonderfully in her book *A Return to Love*, "It's not that we are afraid of our weakness, we are afraid of our greatness." Make living your dreams a priority. Sit down, stop, and don't do anything for a moment. Take time to honor your dreams and honor yourself. Simply ask, what do your (dreams) require? What do your (dreams) want?

Spend time at least every other day and check in with your dreams. What are they doing? What do they want? What do they require? There are a lot of different methods you can use to check in. You can brainstorm with yourself. You can work with a dream partner. Sit down with a pen and paper and write down whatever comes to your mind. Let the pen write whatever it wants to write concerning your dreams.

Your dreams may want to take a little different path. Your dreams may really just want to be expressed and shared. There is no right or wrong way. There is just doing or not doing. You can meditate, visualize, imagine, or contemplate about your dreams. Any of these practices will enable you to have an awareness of what your dreams may want and require.

When you take the time and effort to be with your dreams, you may determine a different path to take to achieve them. You may discover new methods to expand your dreams. What would your dreams want and require if you couldn't fail? Ask and you might just receive what you asked for.

The method I use to allow ideas to flow is a form of free writing. I take out a blank piece of paper and write the subject in the middle of the page and circle it. All around that subject or dream, I write without thought whatever the pen wants to write.

In the case of my dream to complete this book, I wrote, *The Dream Catcher*, and thought, what does my dream of completing this book need and require? And then I allowed the pen to do whatever it wanted. The result was the chapters and subjects for this book. This technique will help you give your dreams the attention they deserve and will help them to become a reality.

You were told as a kid not to daydream. They said that daydreaming is a waste of time. I'm saying to get over it. Go ahead and daydream. Daydreaming is beneficial to the attainment, formulation, and refinement of your dreams. I say, daydream. I encourage it, particularly right before you go to bed. Your subconscious mind will create solutions and ideas to help you reach your dreams while you sleep. Keep a pen and pad or a recording device next to your bed so you won't miss any ideas that come.

"It is never too late to be what you might have been."
~George Eliot

Take Your Dreams Everywhere

Simply take them with you. Type them up and put them in your purse, pocket, or wallet. Post them in your bedroom, bathroom, kitchen, in your journal, and even your car. Share your dreams on social media. Your dreams will continually be on your mind consciously and subconsciously. In a short time your dreams will naturally remain on the forefront of your mind. Make it fun, type or write a copy of your dreams, and put it in your shoe or your sock. That way you will feel them and be reminded of your dreams the whole day. You will feel it and say, "What is that?" and then you will reminder and say, "Oh yes, those are my dreams." The note in my sock says:

1. I'm a magnificent husband.
2. I'm married to an amazing, beautiful, talented, intelligent, caring, creative, spiritual woman.
3. My body is in perfect health, vitality, and balance.
4. This book, *Your Dream Catcher,* is finished and helping thousands to realize and live their dreams.

What are your dreams? Health, to start a new career, take a dance class, to find your dream relationship, travel to Spain, or write a book? Write out your dreams and put them in your shoe or sock or under your hat or cap. Put them in your car, your glove box, your pocket. Put your dreams under your pillow. Take them with you wherever you go.

Another place to take your dreams, which is great for your creative mind, is on a vacation. When you go on vacation, you are out of your routine. You don't have that go-go attitude. When you are on vacation, you can get away and not think about all the different things in life, the to do's and have to's, the job, the family, and all your household duties. Vacations are a perfect time to relax and be present with your dreams.

While on vacation is a good time to ask your dreams what they want. Your mind is in a whole other place. You are relaxed, positive, and excited. You have a sense of fun and adventure with a feeling of possibilities and curiosity. Take a journal, or journal in your smart phone while on your trip.

Dream Notes

To Jump-Start Your Dreams

Share your Dreams with a least 2 people in the next

48 Hours!

You can also be present with your dreams when you meditate and get quiet. Take your dreams on a walk or a hike in nature. Most importantly, keep your dreams with you in your mind. Know that your dreams are a priority in your life.

Talk to Your Dreams

Talking to your dreams is giving them life and energy. Be mindful of how you speak about your dreams. You want to be affirmative and positive toward your dreams. Tell your dreams, "I can live my dreams." "I can achieve anything I desire." Stay cautious and avoid negativity. Talk to them like you talk to a friend. Say, "Hey, magnificent husband, I know your perfect match has already found you." Your dreams will respond to your affirmative statements. It has been proven that plants respond to the manner in which someone speaks to them. If talking to plants creates a positive effect, so can talking to your dreams.

I talk to my dream of having this book published. I pronounce, "My book is published." "I'm in the ideal relationship." "I have vibrant energy." "My level of fitness is amazing." This works for me. My dreams are constantly and continually on my mind. By tending to my dreams daily and staying in a conversation with them, I'm moving closer to them each and every day. Keep your dreams on your mind by taking the time to talk to your dreams.

Be Flexible with Your Dreams

Don't be hung up on exactly what your dreams should look like or how they should come about. You may be aiming too low. Your dreams are likely much bigger than you imagine. Your dreams might go in a completely different direction than you considered. Be flexible. Even when you aim high enough and have your best dream in mind, there are countless corrections and adjustments to make along the way. The realization of your dreams can be like a ship captain who is plotting a course. A ship captain is continually correcting as they are navigating their journey. It is the same for an airline pilot on a flight from Los Angeles to New York. They may make 1,000 to 2,000 tiny corrections on their course during the flight. You can do the same thing with your dreams; be flexible and ready to make many small corrections along your journey.

Allow your dreams to guide you. For me to have perfect health, a published book, and be in an amazing relationship, there can be many adjustments along the way. I may shift to a different health practitioner, a new diet, exercise program, or to a new type of vitamins, or no vitamins. I may want to work on clearing my emotions and to learn to relax more deeply. It will serve me to be open to new things, methods, and ideas. Another way to be flexible is to continue to learn, study, read, and gather new information. Talk to experts. Learn from people who have already achieved your dream. Model what they did. Ask questions, and ask for advice. What were their major course corrections? How did they do it? And why? What was their greatest obstacle? What was their breakthrough moment? How did they get to it? How did they recognize that moment? And what did it take to believe it?

Utilize Google to the fullest. Google everything related to your dreams. Record everything in your journal. Constantly check in with your goals and dreams. Are you still passionate? Do you want to go another direction? Are you even more excited than yesterday? This information allows you to course-correct more directly for your dreams.

> "Some people say there's nothing new under the sun. I still think that there's room to create, you know. And intuition doesn't necessarily come from under this sun. It comes from within."
>
> ~Pharrell Williams

For example, to help me with my goal of getting married, I have a goal of learning to be more comfortable talking to women. I practice talking to everyone and anyone. I don't allow my pride or ego to get in the way. I'm flexible in the methods I'm learning on conversation and confidence. I'm ready to try something new and different.

Do at Least One Thing a Day (OTAD)

Often your Heckler will make things much more difficult than they are. As stated in chapter three, the Heckler over-complicates things, intensifies, modifies, and encourages you to procrastinate and provides you with multiple distractions. No matter what, even if you are sick, even if you have to visit someone in the hospital, work overtime, or have to cook, do the groceries, and the dishes, there is always time to do just one thing! As my good friend and mentor Mary Berg calls it, OTAD (one thing a day), even if it's to send one text. You could, in less than a minute, jot down some ideas, thoughts, or possibilities for a particular dream. You could read a few pages in a book related to one of your dreams. You could call a friend for feedback or work on one of the exercises in this book.

If you do just one thing every day...that's 365 things done in just one year. In ten years, that's 3,650 tasks, steps, or accomplishments completed toward a life that matters. That's 3,650 steps closer to your dream life.

When you do one thing, it just might lead to another, and then another. When you have the momentum and the gift of starting, it is much easier to do more. OTAD thus has the additional benefit of getting you moving daily toward your dreams. With the potential of moving toward your dreams, you just might do more.

OTAD has another wonderful side effect. When you start taking steps, even if it's just one a day you will start to believe in yourself and your dreams. You will realize a real possibility that you can and will have a life that you love, a life where your dreams will come true. As you believe in your dreams, you believe in yourself. By doing just one thing a day, you can transform your life.

You will begin to believe that you do indeed matter. You'll realize you are connected to everything. You'll know that something bigger than yourself wants you to succeed and realize your dreams. When you come to know this truth, your dreams will start to come alive. As you step toward your dreams your dreams step toward you. What an incredible benefit, and all you have to do is one thing.

> "Intuition is a spiritual faculty and does not explain, but simply points the way."
> ~Florence Scovel Shinn

Call Your Dream Buddy

Search your thoughts for someone you like and trust, someone who has a similar motivation to improve, succeed, and to reach their goals and dreams like you do! Think of friends, relatives, co-workers, someone from the gym, yoga, church, or the spiritual center. Make a list and look it over. Ask your intuition to help you choose the right person to be your dream partner or buddy (see chapter eight). Check in on how it feels when you think of each one on your list as your potential dream partner. Then call the person whom your intuition guided you to and ask them if he or she would like to share their dreams with you. If they seem interested, great; if not, go to the next person on your list.

Once you find your buddy, set a time and you can meet up on the phone, or better, in person. Share your dreams and why you chose them. Explain the steps you plan on taking to reach your dreams. Tell your buddy one thing you did or will do today that will move you closer to one of your dreams. Have your partner do the same. You will be amazed how much you will learn by hearing your partner talk about their dreams. You will help each other build structure, confidence, and momentum.

It's important to be willing to share everything, to be vulnerable. You might say, "I didn't do one thing today, and this is why I feel a little bit afraid." There is healing in being authentic and honest. Your partner can offer support and encouragement so tomorrow will be a bit easier for you to fulfill your OTAD. Your buddy can encourage you to write that one thing down and motivate you to do it. When you need help, don't be afraid to call your buddy. Encourage them to call you for support. Remember, there is nothing more important than your dreams.

Nurture Your Dreams

Take care of your dreams. Honor them. Write your dreams in your journal. Make your writing beautiful, positive, and full of possibilities. Buy the best journal you can find. Your dreams are worth it. Write your dreams in your journal and add whatever art or mixed media that most moves you. Allow your inner artist to come out.

The process doesn't have to be complicated. Simply love your dreams enough to create a visual for it. Treat your dreams as you would treat your child. In truth, your dreams are your children. Look after, nurture, and encourage your dreams, just as you would look after, nurture, and encourage a real child. Give your dreams everything they need. Guard them. Look after them, and most of all, love them.

Be careful who you share your dreams with. If you do share them with someone other than your coach or dream partner, make sure they are someone who will be supportive. Don't share them with a stranger or someone who may be negative.

When I was taking a public speaking class, the teacher thought my speech about 9/11 was so impactful she had me share it with another class she was teaching. I was so excited thinking, I'm going to be a professional public speaker. The teacher even said, "I couldn't give that speech on that subject as well as David."

Catch your dreams	**Nurture**
	* care for
	* encourage the growth or development of
	* help or encourage the development of
	Merriam-Webster

I shared the experience with a woman in a class at the spiritual center I attended and added that I was going to be a public speaker. The woman said, "It's almost impossible to be a professional public speaker. I know of someone who is excellent, with years of experience and training. He has an equally positive and spiritual view on life as you, David. And my friend can't make a living public speaking." My dream was crushed. I couldn't get her words out of my mind. I gave up the dream for over eight years. Eight years I will never have back to work toward my dream. Guard and nurture your dreams every day.

Celebrate Your Dreams

Celebrate every single step. When you move closer to one of your dreams, celebrate. When you enroll and complete a class, celebrate. When you start writing and then finish an outline or rough draft of your book, celebrate. When you go out and buy your dream journal, celebrate. Celebrate all your accomplishments, all of your steps forward, all of your efforts! Call your coach or dream buddy and let them know. Buy yourself a dessert, go to the movies, walk in nature, treat yourself to whatever makes you happy. Go to bed excited. Wake up excited. Celebrate every action you take every day. You just moved closer to realizing your dream. Yes, that is a big deal, and yes, it is a really good thing.

"It is better to risk starving to death then surrender. If you give up on your dreams, what's left?"
~Jim Carrey

Love Your Dreams

When you love something, you pay attention to it. When you love your dreams, you will be motivated and inspired to do something towards achieving your dreams every day. Every day you can make at least one phone call. Every day you can write, paint, draw, or dance. Every day you can learn something new about being a better husband, wife, writer, painter, or dancer. Every day, you can love your dreams.

Start believing your dreams will come true. Believe and know you are worthy. Start to love yourself and your dreams more and more every day. Make sure your behaviors and habits are in alignment with your dreams. By loving them, it will be natural to do the things necessary to foster, nurture, and make sure your dreams thrive. You will love your dreams the same as you would love your own child— because they are.

Conclusion

When you wake up in the morning, tell yourself, *"I'm tending to my dreams today."* There is nothing more important than tending to your dreams to ensure their completion. Give yourself and your dreams the time and space required for their completion. Make sure you ask them what they need. Talk to them and take them everywhere you go.

Remember to be flexible and allow your dreams to change direction, to expand, and grow in ways you may have not originally intended. By doing just one thing a day toward your dreams, you will have taken 365 steps toward your dreams in just one year. Find a dream partner to help you love, celebrate, and nurture your dreams. Know that you and your dreams are worth the effort. Realize that your life and your dreams matter. By truly understanding that you and your dreams matter you will automatically, *tend to your dreams daily.*

DREAMS
COME
TRUE

Recap — Tend to Your Dreams Daily

Make Time and Space for Your Dreams: make your dreams your number-one priority.

Dream Breakdown Structure: a set of blueprints for your dreams.

Ask Your Dreams What They Want and What They Require: take the time to consider the most important thing in your life, your dreams.

Take Your Dreams Everywhere: put them in your smart phone, purse, or wallet and view them often.

Talk to Your Dreams: talking to your dreams gives them life.

Be Flexible with Your Dreams: don't worry about how exactly your dreams should look.

Do at Least One Thing a Day (OTAD): one thing a day is 365 in a year.

Call Your Dream Buddy: sharing helps create the reality of your dreams.

Nurture Your Dreams: take care and honor your dreams.

Celebrate Your Dreams: give yourself credit and reward yourself for you accomplishments.

Love Your Dreams: love your dreams like you would your own child — because they are.

Dreamtime
Do Try This at Home

1. Post your top three dreams and behaviors in your bedroom, bathroom, kitchen, and in your car. List your top three dreams in your journal. Read them aloud at least once every day (see appendix #8).

2. Go to bed ready...this means go to bed ready to work on your dreams first thing when you wake up. Have all your materials and information in order and ready to go. Start your mornings by doing at least one thing, first thing when you wake up.

3. Carry your dream journal with you this entire week. At least three times a day, playfully write in your journal. Note how wonderful it is to have your dreams to work toward. Jot down any ideas, inspirations, or what you want to do next. Write about what you may be concerned about, and/or where you may need more knowledge or skills. Make it a game to make at least one notation daily.

4. Keep your dreams in mind. Make them your dominant thought. Wear a rubber band around your wrist to remind

you about your dreams. Keep your journal in a place where you can see it. Constantly read and reread your dreams. Think about your dreams as often and as much as possible.

Declaration:

From now on, I will tend to my dreams daily!

Your

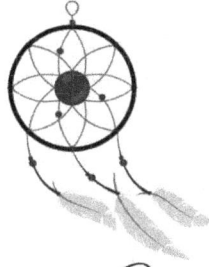

DREAM CATCHER

Chapter VIII. Follow your Intuition

"By learning to contact, listen to, and act on our intuition, we can directly connect to the higher power of the universe and allow it to become our guiding force."

~Shakti Gawain

Imagine yourself possessing the ability to make the best choices and decisions in all aspects of your life. Because of your intuition, you are already divinely connected to all the information that life has to offer. Your intuition will guide you to the life of your dreams. Intuition is the spark, the seed, the information that leads you to your passions, creativity, goals, wisdom, and dreams.

Imagine the joy you will feel as you follow the steps toward your dreams. When you learn to listen, intuition will provide you the wisdom and information you need to live your dreams. You were born with the capacity to receive the divine guidance of intuition. This gift called intuition will transform your life.

Your desire to catch your dreams calls you to seek information and guidance. With your next easy breath, you can begin to create an avenue for insights, ideas, and inspiration to be received. Your desire to live your dreams coupled with relaxing into the hope and expectation to live an amazing life calls intuition into your awareness.

The *Oxford English Dictionary* defines intuition as, "The quick perception of truth without conscious attention or reasoning; Knowledge from within; Instinctive knowledge, or feeling." The first thing that pops into your mind is usually your intuition. If it's instant, you can count on it being intuition. You know it is intuition when it's an immediate, spontaneous thought or insight. Your intuition is that first guess on a test or the first name that comes to mind when meeting someone for the second time. The next, or second guess, is from your intellect, not your intuition. When you have a choice between intuition and intellect, choose intuition.

Intuition is like having a personal advisor who knows everything about you, your situation, and the world. Your advisor, when asked and listened to, will provide you with valuable wisdom and information to assist you toward your dreams. Joel Arthur Barker wrote about intuition in his book *The Power of Decision*: "It is the ability to make good decisions with incomplete data." That is exactly what intuition is. Intuition is knowing something without all the information. When asked for, received, and acted on, intuition can make your life much easier and joyous. With intuition you are able to skip through life's difficulties, problems, and decisions with an assuredness that everything will turn out fine.

You may tend to discount intuition and its wisdom. In today's society, you are often too busy to stop and receive it. You overlook your intuition because of your belief that it's somehow evil, foreign, or unreliable. Perhaps you just don't know about or believe in intuition. Intuition is a natural experience you have access to. Intuition is a gift you are free to use anytime you choose. It is up to you and to what degree you take advantage of it. Intuition is an amazing tool to support the realization of your goals and dreams.

> **"Belief consists in accepting the affirmations of the soul; unbelief, in denying them."**
> **~Ralph Waldo Emerson**

Intuition is Essential

Cavemen and cavewomen had to use their intuition for survival. Every time they came out of their cave, there was danger everywhere. Often, even their cave wasn't safe. To survive, they tuned in to their intuition. It was a matter of life or death! Where is the food? Is it food, and is it edible? Where are the saber-tooth tigers, the carnivorous dinosaurs? Are there other cave people nearby who are even hungrier? Intuition was more than essential to our ancestors; it was a matter of life or death!

Today we don't need intuition for survival, but it's essential to thrive. With intuition you can make better decisions in all areas of life. It aids in problem solving, decision making, goals, dream making and their realization.

Intuition is Often Not Developed

Unfortunately, much of Western society frowns on intuition. An example is daydreaming. Daydreaming is one of the actions you were taught to avoid in school. Our teachers, parents, and society place a high priority on staying focused. That poor kid who continually got caught and punished for daydreaming was simply honing his intuition skills.

The greatest example of a kid who didn't get the best grades, who daydreamed and used his intuition skills, was Albert Einstein. His intuition helped him become known as one of the greatest minds in history. Everything starts with an idea or thought. Ideas and thoughts come from imagination and intuition.

Daydreaming is a form or platform for us to develop our intuition. Walter Isaacson in his book *Einstein: His Life and Universe* wrote, "Einstein's ability to do what he called thought experiments is how Einstein was able to give birth to many of his theories." A thought experiment is a type of daydreaming. Einstein formed images with pictures of events in his mind. Dr. Einstein would then run his theory in his mind to see if the idea was correct. One such thought experiment Einstein worked on was to determine what would happen to time as someone was traveling at the speed of light. Amazingly, as we know, many of Einstein's thought experiments, or his daydreaming, were later proven correct.

In school and growing up, we were constantly told to pay attention, to keep our minds focused. If we were caught daydreaming, we were reprimanded, made fun of, and often received detention for it. What made things worse was the fact the classmates made fun of us, or so we believed. Our fear of shame and the embarrassment of being caught doing something wrong was motivation enough to stop. There are few things worse for a child in school than to be made fun of by their classmates. That sure stopped me from daydreaming. I never imagined I was stifling the fulfillment of my dreams by not daydreaming.

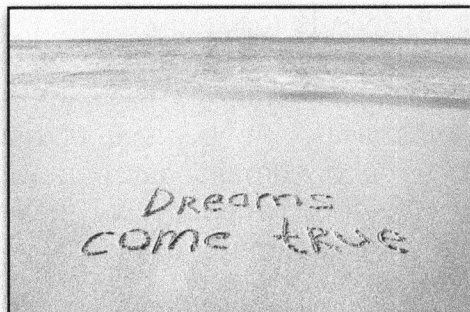

Daydream

* a series of pleasant thought that distract one's attention

* a vision

* a found hope

Merriam-Webster

Daydreaming, or intuition, is extremely valuable in helping you reach your dreams. It would be difficult if not impossible to connect with your true heart's desire without the ability to daydream. It's something you can use in all areas of your life. Without daydreaming how can you know what your dreams are? How would you make a chart or imagine what being coachable is like, trusting our fears, or loving your body?

There are several more factors why we don't develop our gift of intuition. Primarily they are society, religious beliefs, and fear. We often don't see the benefits. Many of us just don't realize the gift that intuition is. We have no idea that our intuition is a gateway or bridge for you to live the life you want and to catch your dreams. Following your intuition is a major step in forming and making your dreams come true.

In today's busy material world there is little time or thought of intuition. Consumerism is what drives us. Our time, thoughts, and efforts are devoted to acquiring more and more. When we have more things, we then turn our attention to how we are going to keep them. Our time and energy are focused on image. We focus on how we look and what are the latest fashions. We are concerned about where we live, what make and model car we drive, do we own the latest and best cell phone, computer, and how flat is our television. In short, we are simply too busy, and our concerns are directed elsewhere. Our lifestyle is focused outside the inner self, where intuition lives. Judee Gee, in her book *Intuition: Awakening Your Inner Guide,* writes, "Our image is more important than our authenticity." As a result of our busyness in trying to keep up and surpass our parents, neighbors, and keep up with the Joneses, we have neglected our intuition and often our dreams.

The Western education system is linear-based, focused on math, history, writing, and reading. We are trained at an early age not to use the creative right side of our brains. I believe it is best to be balanced in everything, including developing your creative nature. In school there are few, if any, classes that even refer to your creativity, imagination, or intuition.

Fear of the unknown and uncertainty of the unseen have fostered our fears. For many, learning we have an invisible inner power is considered evil and something to avoid. This goes back to the foundation of our religions and social influences.

Our ancestors were taught that these evil spirits could enter our minds and control us. Not too long ago many thought that any sort of power, even the power of intuition, was somehow demonic and sinful. Today you may not consciously believe intuition is evil. Unfortunately, the teachings of your ancestors are often deeply rooted into your subconscious. Unconsciously, you may not want anything to do with a power that seems to be wrong or outside of yourself.

American culture has taught you to be self-sufficient. You strive to be independent of outside influences. Information (even wise information) coming out of seemingly nowhere can be something you simply refuse.

Most are too busy to think about intuition. Lifestyles are much faster and more involved than they were in past times and generations. You have many more distractions with TV, emails, computers, cell phones, text messages, Internet, Facebook, and Twitter. Many have more than one job. School, kids, the gym, and grocery shopping is all you can keep up with. With your busy lifestyle, it is unlikely you can detect intuition in your life. By the time you do slow down, you are too tired to listen!

> **"The only real valuable thing is intuition."**
> **~Albert Einstein**

Intuition, imagination, and your ability to visualize need to be practiced. Nancy Rosanoff in her book, *Intuition Workout,* explained, "Intuition is like a muscle. It needs exercise to become strong, flexible, and reliable." You need to exercise and practice receiving and then follow your intuition. With practice, by completing the Dreamtime exercises at the end of the chapter, you will be able to receive your inner gift of intuition.

For me, I didn't understand nor could I see the benefits of using my intuition. Without fully using my intuition and imagination, I didn't have a vivid picture of my dreams. I didn't understand that without using my intuition, I wouldn't be able to determine or achieve my dreams. By understanding the benefits and why you haven't taken advantage of your intuition and imagination, you can stop running and make a conscious choice to develop and use your intuition to determine and catch your dreams.

Dream Notes

To Jump-Start Your Dreams

Simply choose your Dreams
say to yourself
"Today I choose my Dreams"

Stop Running From Intuition

What stop running means is to slow down, take a moment, sit still, and listen. Devote a few minutes a day to hear your intuition. Being alone with yourself for many can be frightening. You could be afraid that somehow if you slow down and stop running, you might discover for yourself that you aren't as wonderful as you thought. Somehow you think that by running, no one, including yourself, will find out.

The more you run, the more you feel the need to run. This is why, as a society, we drink, take drugs, overeat, watch too much TV, participate in and watch sports, over work, and over exercise. People do these mind-numbing activities to escape. They are terrified to examine themselves. To look inside is often frightening. To tap into your higher intuitive self may seem too weird. It is time to get over your misconceptions. If you want to catch your dreams, intuition is mandatory.

The problem is that you have to make an effort to access and follow your intuition. Intuition doesn't come by and knock you on the head. Intuition is rather subtle and quiet. It can be a feeling, emotion, thought, something you hear or see. Intuition can come as a coincidence, synchronicity, or a perception. You simply have to stop running to receive the gift of intuition.

People run for all kinds of reasons. They don't want to feel their emotions. They are fearful they will find out God doesn't love them or that there might not even be a God at all. For me, I was afraid that I would find out that I wasn't enough. I was afraid to discover that I might not be worthy of God's love, or anybody's love. Somehow being still and quiet would tell me and announce to the world that I was somehow broken beyond repair.

With all the fears listed above, it's understandable why we can be reluctant to slow down. We fear we are already a failure with no chance for redemption. We act as if failure is a permanent condition. What happens if we don't receive any intuition, or what if it isn't any good? Would that mean we aren't connected to the Divine? If we aren't connected to God, then there must be something terribly wrong with us! I know that's something I didn't want to know about.

Once I understood that everyone has equal access to the Divine, God, and therefore to intuition. I got that intuition was part of the way things work. Intuition is natural and normal. I realized all inventions, from the wheel to the toaster, were first an idea originating from intuition. With this understanding, I was able to slow down, allow, trust myself, and trust in the process of listening for and then following my intuition.

There are dozens of ways you can receive intuition. You can see it, hear it, dream it, feel or sense it, or just know it. Sitting still is one method, perhaps the most efficient, and certainly not the only. The biggest problem with sitting still is for us to simply do it.

I never seemed to find the time to stop, sit down, and see what might come. I would make it the last item on my to-do list rather than the first. Sitting still was a big problem for me until my friend Richard came up with a great plan. He calls it the one-minute meditation. (To me and for the purposes of this book, sitting still and listening for my intuition is very similar to meditation.) Richard suggested that I sit and meditate just for a minute, that's it. I can always meditate or sit in stillness for one minute. Richard says if I wanted, if it felt okay, I could sit for another minute or two. The idea is to just start. Once you are there, it's easy to extend the time. A commitment for one minute is easy. There is nothing terrifying about sixty seconds. You can find the time to sit just for a minute.

Using the one-minute meditation, or the sitting-still practice, will help you *Dare to Dream,* and then *Chart Our Dreams.* Be still, receptive, and open to what may come to you. Have a journal and pen ready to record all that comes to you.

You can stop running as you realize you are human. You stop because, what choice do you have? At some point you are going to have to look at your life. You have to come to terms with your humanity, and your imperfections. You might as well do it now. Sitting, or meditating, is the most important thing you can do for yourself. When you stop running and be still, you will tune into the guidance of your intuition.

Just like the dishes. You might as well do it now. It's only going to be more difficult later. It's perfectly fine to use the one minute meditation. With success, sitting will become easier. When you start to receive intuitive flashes of insight and information, getting quiet and sitting will become fun and exciting.

> **"Faith is a passionate intuition."**
> **~William Wordsworth**

Where Does Intuition Come From?

Sonia Choquette, Ph.D., in her book *Your Heart's Desire*, expresses to her readers, "It's easier to train your senses to notice your intuition if you have an understanding where those intuitive flashes originate." Dr. Choquette goes on to explain that, "If you are going to convince your mind to listen to your intuitive feelings, your mind has to value those feelings." If you know and value the sense of our intuitive guidance, you are more likely to listen and act on it. An example would be in making a financial investment. If you didn't know and had never heard of the person giving you advice, how positive would you be? On the other hand, how would you feel if the other person advising you was your favorite sister-in-law who graduated top of her class with a doctorate from the Harvard School of Finance?

Many consider intuition to be a mystery. Intuition seems to be mysterious because we can't see or touch it. Even skeptics of intuition experience it to some degree almost every day. Intuition comes as a feeling, a thought, or a hunch that something is right or not right. You have heard the expression, women's intuition. I'll never forget my mother's intuition. This is a true story about the one and only time I stole candy from a store. I came home, and my mother sat me down and lectured me about stealing and how bad, shameful, and wrong it was. How was it that she knew? The one and only time I stole something. It had to be woman's, or mother's intuition.

One of the ways you receive intuition is from your subconscious mind. Your subconscious mind takes in huge amounts of information every second. Only a small fraction of this information reaches your conscious mind. If your conscious mind took in all the information, it would be too much for us to process. Your subconscious mind has downloaded and stored all this information just like a giant computer. This information is available and waiting to be used. An example of this is how someone can give vivid details, under hypnosis, of events they had consciously forgotten in their childhood.

When I was a waiter serving tables, I was amazed at the power of my subconscious mind. I could remember all the details of up to ten tables at once. I knew where in their meal each table was, what they needed, and in what sequence. I planned every move five to ten minutes in the future. With ten tables and over thirty-five customers, that is a lot of information to sort through. As I returned change for one table, I turned in a ticket for another, served salads, a dessert, and a Coke to three different tables, all with one trip to the kitchen. Being extra busy activated my subconscious mind into action. I could better serve ten tables with the help of my subconscious mind than two with just my conscious mind.

Another way we receive intuition is through telepathy. The *American Oxford Dictionary* explains telepathy to be Greek, *tele* meaning "distant," and *patheia* meaning "to be affected by". Telepathy refers to the transfer of information on thoughts or feelings between individuals by means other than the five classical senses. You have heard and experienced the phrase, "He or she just gave me the wrong vibe." That is exactly it. It's the vibe or vibration that you felt and experienced. It can come strictly from vibration, or more likely, it's the overall impression you received from the person. Not only vibrations but how they looked, acted, the pitch, sound, and volume of their voice, and how they smelled. All of this information went into your perception that this person was someone you might or might not like to interact with.

The more external and internal clues you can gather, the better decision you can make. That's why meditation, sitting, or relaxation is so important. Slowing down to listen to your intuition provides you with more information to make better decisions.

A perfect example happened to me the other day. My old accountant tripled his prices. Naturally, I thought I would try someone else. My banker recommended a large franchised company I won't name. The office was pleasant enough. It was clean, with the entire front taken up by a clear, clean window providing lots of light. The receptionist was pleasant and attentive. There was a couple that looked like they were finishing up with their appointment and another couple waiting next to me. In the office there were six desks, three on each side. Before I met with my tax preparer, I went to the bathroom. When I came back, an older man dressed rather ordinary said, "I will be right with you." The poor man had a crooked eye. In that instant I couldn't figure out which eye was the dominant eye. I was unable to discern if he was talking to me or his colleague at the desk behind me. That was my first intuitive clue. If I don't know where he is looking, how will I know if he is looking after my best interest with my taxes?

Then he called me to his desk. He asked to see my last year's tax returns. I gave him a copy on a disk. He made no effort to hide his displeasure that they were not on paper.

He stomped to the back room. Then he couldn't get the disk to open on his computer. Then he said my disk messed up the computer, and he would have to reboot the entire system.

Catch your dreams

Imagination

* the act or power of forming a mental image of something not present to the senses or never before wholly perceived in reality

* creative ability

* ability to confront and deal with a problem

Merriam-Webster

That was enough for me. Amazingly, as I excused myself, the secretary confirmed the situation by saying, "Got the wrong vibe!" It was said as more of a statement than a question. If I had listened to my intuition, I wouldn't have made the appointment. I had plenty of information when I scheduled the appointment. I called for the appointment late in the afternoon on April 11th. They asked me what day and time I wanted to come in. Four days before tax day and I could come in anytime I wanted! I should have saved myself the trouble and said thanks but no thanks.

The best answer to the question where intuition comes from is a higher Source. God created the entire universe and everything in it. Spirit gave us life. You have your body to move and your brain to think. If God made everything, if God gave us so many gifts, why would it be so hard to consider that God could give us the gift of intuition? Intuition, when applied, makes life much easier. You can have the gift of making the best choices in your life: who to marry, where to live, your perfect occupation, your purpose in life. If God made everything, then God made intuition too. It comes by way of our subconscious, your connection with God.

Intuition also comes from what Carl Jung called the collective unconscious, the universal knowledge of all man-women-kind. It is believed by many, including Jung, that it is possible through intuition to tap into all the knowledge and wisdom of man- women-kind. As Jung put it, "A reservoir of the experiences of our species." It's that part we don't normally access, but with understanding, practice, and patience, we can.

Great thinkers, including Thomas Edison and Albert Einstein, were able to receive their discoveries through intuition. They both used a similar method to gain access. They found that in-between the state of not fully awake and not fully asleep is where they could best access their intuition. They would think of a problem that needed a solution. Then they would sit down in a chair with something heavy in their hands like ball bearings, and then they would allow themselves to drift off to sleep. At the moment when they would fall asleep, the heavy objects would fall out of their hands and wake them up, precisely at that moment between sleep and waking consciousness. This moment between being awake and asleep is where they accessed their intuition. Einstein and Edison would often wake up with an insight transforming their stumbling block into a solution.

After Einstein's death, research was performed on his brain. Einstein didn't speak until he was older than normal for a child to speak. The part of his brain that causes speech was underdeveloped, but the creative area where he could see pictures and dream was more developed, enabling him to be considered the greatest mind of the twentieth century. Many of his discoveries were created simply by daydreaming.

Once you put a question out there, the Divine begins to bring you solutions. It can assist you in methods, ways, and ideas, on how to earn your GED, how to interview to win a McDonald's franchise, or how to be a model husband and more.

"Every great dream begins with a dreamer. Always remember, you have within you the strength, the patience, and the passion to reach for the stars to change the world."
~Harriet Tubman

How You Receive Intuition

Intuition comes to you simply as a knowing. You just know something to be true or false, right or wrong. Intuition can come as an inner vision in your mind's eye. An idea, a flash of inspiration, or a belief are all forms of intuition. To daydream is a form of inner vision, imagination, or intuition. Much of intuition comes as a feeling in your body. Often you hear the expression, "I felt it in my gut." It can come as a tightness in your chest, a feeling of satisfaction in your stomach, or a pain in the neck. Intuition can also be sensed as a warm, comfortable feeling. People often say that a decision, job, home, or mate just felt right. Some people hear insights or advice in their inner ear.

Intuition can come to you as synchronicity and coincidences. When you consider the possibility that synchronicity and coincidences are for your benefit, you'll begin to be more aware of them. Note in your journal how the synchronicity and coincidence that come into your life support your dreams. Synchronicity and coincidences can come from lyrics in a song, a billboard, anything on the radio or television, a conversation, and in an infinite variety of sources. Insight can come from anywhere. The next word you hear could contain an answer you are looking for.

Intuition can come as an inner knowing that something is right. You know that a McDonald's franchise is right for you. You are confident that completing your GED is your best option. You can also be informed if something or someone isn't good for you to be around.

Imagination the Language of Intuition

Einstein stated, "Logic will get you from A to B. Imagination will take you everywhere," and "Imagination is everything. It is more important than knowledge. It is the preview of life's coming attractions." Imagination is just one of many forms of intuition. Imagination is the ability to form images and ideas in the mind, especially things not experienced or seen directly. Imagination is the place where ideas, thoughts, and images are formed.

You can use your intuition through your imagination, your mind's eye. For example, Jeremy can use imagination to help his schoolwork. He can use imagination to select a topic to write about and craft a paper. Michelle can imagine, visualize, and practice the interview process prior to the actual interview. She can use her imagination to determine what to say, how to respond, and what to wear. Michelle can choose what skills and experience to share and what questions to ask. Imagination is extremely helpful when choosing a mate, friend, or business partner. You can utilize intuition to choose what qualities are most important to strengthen and develop to become a great husband or wife.

Dream Notes

To Jump-Start Your Dreams

Before you go to sleep declare one thing you will do the next day to better the world.

Know Yourself

In her book *Awakening Intuition,* Frances E. Vaughan wrote, "Only when you are willing to be wide awake to the reality of who you are, to confront your fears and see the truth of yourself, can you be truly open to the many levels of the intuitive experience." Intuition will open you up to discover who you are. It will guide you to know how you really think and feel. When you know yourself on a deeper level, you can better harness your intuition. Understanding yourself will help give you the confidence to explore your intuitive nature and determine what to focus on.

When you fully discover your deepest feelings, you begin to know your true values, motivations, and desires. Only by fully knowing your deepest feelings and desires can you determine your authentic goals and dreams. Without authentic dreams that match who you really are, you may never achieve your heart's desires.

You can start to know yourself by looking within to your true nature. You need to take the risk to feel all of your feelings, exposing yourself to your true self. Without knowing your true self, your gift of intuition will be ineffective.

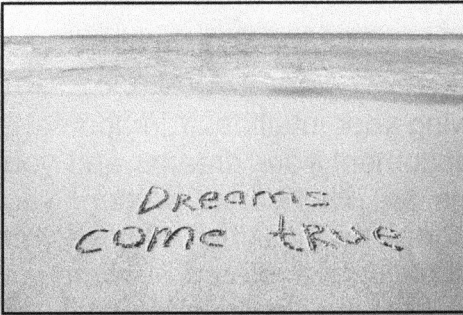

Meditation

* to engage in contemplation or reflection

* to engage in mental exercise (such as concentration on one's breathing or repetition of a mantra) for the purpose of reaching a heightened level of spiritual awareness

* to focus one's thoughts on

* reflect on or ponder over

Merriam-Webster

Be Still

You can call it meditation, sitting, or just relaxing. Whatever you call it, you need to relax your body and mind to best experience your intuition. When you are at ease, intuition will come to you. Give intuition a chance by creating an environment for it to occur. Einstein would just think of a project he wanted to solve or improve and simply take a nap, play the violin, or go for a long walk.

If your mind is busy, intuition has no space to inter your consciousness. In your hectic keep-up-with-the-Joneses lifestyle, you can find it difficult to sit still. Your intuition won't come to you as easily unless you create a space and time for it to arrive. Simply by being still you create the necessary time and space. Still means motionless, quiet time for your mind and body. The amount of time is up to you. It is the same as with most things; the more time you give it, the better the results.

Keep a Journal

Journaling is crucial in following your intuition. Your journal is a space holder for you to document your dreams and your intuition. When your dreams are stated and written, your intuition can begin creating ideas and insights to make your dreams real. Your journal will become a reference where you can record your progress. Include in your journal the insights, revelations, and information your intuition has given you to make your dreams a reality.

You will also want to have a separate journal for your nighttime dreams. Judith Orloff, in her book *Intuitive Healing,* states, "Your dreams are one of the best places we receive intuitive guidance every night." Keep your nighttime journal by your bed with a pen or pencil. Write down your dreams as soon as you wake up. Don't wait until breakfast to write them. You will often forget the insight if you do. I would suggest you buy a book on dream symbolism and the meanings of dreams to help you interpret your insights.

One of my dreams is to get married. I wrote out my intent, "To find, court, and then marry my soulmate." Then I asked my intuition to give me information to help me. I recorded the insights, information, and ideas in my journal. I then wrote out a plan and timetable to implement those insights. Then I documented in my journal how things worked out. I recorded what worked and didn't work, what I learned, as well as what adjustments I made along the way.

You can also use your journal to write your thoughts and feelings. It is very cathartic to allow yourself to express your feelings. Write about how you feel about your intuition. How are your dreams doing? Do you feel you are on the right track? What adjustments do you intend to make? Are your dreams in alignment with your heart's desires?

Pay attention and have a separate place in your journal to note the synchronicity and coincidences that come into your life. Pay attention to the events that come into your life in an unusual and/or remarkable way. The important thing is to dare to dream, and then chart your journey. This practice will open the door for your intuition to blossom.

Conclusion

Intuition is very important for you to determine and live your dreams. Intuition is pivotal for every chapter of your life and for the formulation and completion of your dreams. It is an insight and a tool to stimulate your mind as creative thought. Intuition is something that stimulates your mind. Use your intuition to move toward your dreams. Intuition is like fuel for the soul.

As you start to realize you are an intuitive being, you can more easily accept the gifts from the unseen. You can open up and go past the fear and become more of who you are. The gifts of intuition will become exponential, where you will have more and more creative ideas, insights, and clarity. More people will come into your life to help you. There will be more synchronicity in your life. Intuition is simply the greatest and most important tool you have for the realization of your dreams.

Recap — Follow your Intuition

Intuition is Essential: it aids in problem solving, decision making, goals, dream making and their realization.

Intuition is Often Not Developed: we frequently are more interested in how we look than in our intuition.

Stop Running From Intuition: take the time to simply listen.

Where Does Intuition Come From?: it can be said it literally is a vibration from the Divine.

How You Receive Intuition: it comes as a feeling, something you see, hear, touch taste, or imagine.

Imagination the Language of Intuition: "It is more important than knowledge; it is a preview of life's coming attractions."
~Albert Einstein

Know Yourself: intuition will open you up to discover who you are.

Be Still: open your mind up to create a space for intuition to come to you.

Keep a Journal: it is critical that you keep a record of the intuition that comes to you.

Dreamtime
Do Try This at Home

1. Read to yourself your top three dreams before you go to bed. Do this every night for at least the next twenty-one days. Allow yourself to be inspired and guided from within regarding what's next in moving you toward your dreams. Note what came to you in your journal. Take an action based on the information you received.

2. Make a section for synchronicity in your journal. Note the events, circumstances, and encounters that come into your life to support your dreams. As things line up in your synchronicity section, note how they support you and your dreams. Make sure to, even if it's very small, take an action toward your dreams as a result of the information.

3. For the next few days, don't second-guess yourself. Do the first thing that comes to mind in regards to your dreams (as long as it's safe and legal, for you or others). Act as if you can't fail. Record how the week went for you.

4. When the phone rings, listen to your intuition and ask who you need to speak to next to move closer to your

dreams. Notice if that is the person who called you. If it's not that person who called, ask yourself, how can the person who did call help you reach your dreams? Then ask your intuition how you can assist the person who called you to reach their dreams. If you guessed the right person, WOW, you are already using your intuition!

Declaration: I will fully trust and follow my intuition to fulfill my dreams.

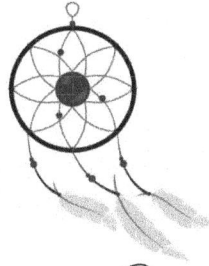

Your

DREAM CATCHER

Chapter IX. Trust your Fears

"The best way out is always through."

~ Helen Keller

What if you could transform your fear to be your friend? What if you trusted your fear and considered it as a tool to help guide and direct you toward your dreams? Fear can help you on your path to go to school, enroll for the class, ask for that date, and to do the things that have held you back. Trust and think of your fears as a guide and a signal, not something to run from but something to ease toward. The Helen Keller quote above stated, "The best way out is always through." To get to where you want to go or who you want to be, fear can be your friend. From this perspective, I don't agree with *Webster's Dictionary's* definition of fear: "Fear is dread along with unpleasant emotion caused by coming evil or danger to shrink from doing something." From the perspective of this chapter, fear is simply information.

There is a common acronym for fear, false evidence appearing real, or false emotion appearing real. I made up a new acronym. **Friends-eliciting-actual-reality**. Fear in this context is unemotional, undifferentiated information serving you as a guide. When taken simply as information, you can act or not act accordingly. Fear is a problem when you give it the power to grow into thoughts and ideas that don't represent reality. Fear is a problem when you magnify your misguided thoughts, and it stops you from action.

It will be much easier when you consider fear as your friend instead of an enemy. Society tends to cartridge things into black and white, good or bad, something to love or often something to fear. Fear is an emotion that most of the time isn't real. It's not about winning or losing, it is about serving and being a contribution. This chapter is about trusting your fears, not running or hiding from them.

> **"The only thing that will stop you from fulfilling your dreams is you."**
> **~Tom Bradley**

Realize That You Are Not Alone

When you realize that you are not the only one, you feel better about your situation. You may think that you are unique to a particular situation, and in reality, you are not. You may believe that your situation is the only situation of its kind. If my friend Janet is deciding to go to medical school and thinks that she is the only one having problems with the application process, she will be more likely to give up. When she realizes that many others are going through exactly what she is going through, Janet will naturally feel better about her situation.

Knowing that other people are experiencing the same things is very beneficial. Realizing you are not alone can also elicit your friends and their friends to teach you how they dealt with their similar situations. In other words, if Janet is having trouble with the medical school application process, she can talk to other people who have already been through it.

Note what fears are present, where and how you are dealing with them, and how others have handled the same difficulties. Know that they were able to learn to trust and deal with their fears. It's helpful in anything that you do to realize that you are not the only one with that experience.

Don't Take Your Fears So Seriously

You tend to take life so seriously that you make such a big deal of your fear that you are paralyzed. You become static and not able to get things done. It's important to enjoy life and not take it so seriously.

Realize that there are no wrong decisions, no wrong way to go. Even when you make a mistake, you learn from it. You learn not to repeat the same mistake again. You learn there is always something to gain from whichever path you choose, even if you think you failed.

Avoid keeping score on how you are progressing toward your dreams. Don't worry about making the perfect decisions. I have been fearful of not being perfect, so I wind up not acting at all. Not realizing that action is better than no action. You wind up being your own jailer, stifling yourself from taking actions toward your dreams.

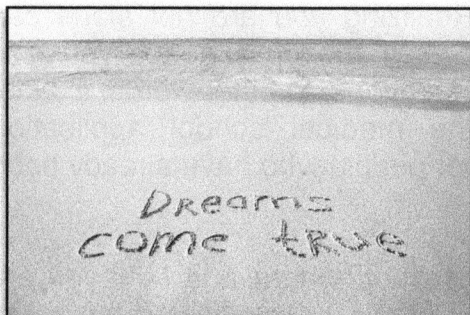

Trust

* assured reliance on the character, ability, strength, or truth of someone or something

* one in which confidence is placed

Merriam-Webster

If you laugh at your fear, it has no power over you. Your mind can only focus on one thing at a time. When you laugh at your fear, your brain will focus on laughing, and in that moment you will forget all about whatever it was you were afraid of.

You learn from your failures. In that respect, a so-called failure is for your own good. The famous quote by Eleanor Roosevelt's husband, Franklin D. Roosevelt, stated, "There's nothing to fear but fear itself," a fear that isn't even real.

Fear can help you to realize your dreams. You can benefit from fear because it tells you that you are on the right track. Fear tells you that you are stretching yourself. When you try something new, that is the time when the fear comes. When you do everything the same today as you did yesterday, when everything is the same, the same people, the same events, you are not going to experience fear. By playing it safe and not expanding, you are not going to grow. Nothing much is going to happen, and you are not going to be any closer to your dreams by living that way.

Say "Yes" To Your Fear

There is something special just when you say, "Yes" to your fear. You are not going to be surprised by feeling fear. Fear will not come onto you like a fog encompassing your whole body. The experience of fear is not going to be a surprise when you accept it by saying "Yes" to it. You will be aware when it comes. You can have fear and be okay with it by accepting and expecting it. By knowing you are not living today exactly as you did yesterday, you are saying "Yes" to your fear. You may be experiencing some fear, and yes, you will be growing as a person and moving closer toward your dreams.

> "We can easily forgive a child who is afraid of the dark; the real tragedy of life is when men are afraid of the light."
> ~Plato

You can reduce your resistance to fear by knowing a spiritual law that states, "What you resist persists." It is natural for human beings to push against something that is pushing them. This applies also in nature. There is a saying in the form of a question that asks, "What is the best way to get the cow out of the barn?" The answer is to push it back in. The cow will resist, and presto, the cow is out of the barn. When there is less resistance to something, as Helen Keller wrote, "You won't even go through it. You will melt with it." Fear can actually be transformed into your friend. It is very important to say, "Yes" to your fear. Start by not resisting it.

Again, realize that fear is most often present when you do something new. There will naturally be some amount of fear because you have never done it before. Don't think you can or should be perfect and/or do everything perfectly. There should be some fear, and it's natural to experience some fear. Saying, "Yes," and by accepting fear will lessen it, allowing you to see the message it is to give you. Say, "Yes" to your fear, and allow it to be your guide.

Realize That Fear Is Your Ally

Fear is your friend. It is a tool to help you live your dream life. Fear is your ally because there are times and things that you should be afraid of. There is real danger out there. Spirit, the Universe, or God didn't give you fear for absolutely no reason. Fear of an accident or death prevents you from driving the wrong way on the freeway. Fear keeps you from running with scissors. Fear is your friend because it will tell you that you are on or off track. If you are doing something new, you will most likely experience some fear. You want to live your dreams and have a life that matters and to contribute to society and yourself. If you want to be a doctor, go on a vacation, own your own home, have a romantic relationship, or to get a new job, the more fear you experience, the closer you will be to realizing your dream.

When you are really going for your dreams, you will experience what I call, *the edge*. A certain amount of fear and uneasiness means you are pushing and moving forward. When on the edge, you aren't too afraid, just enough to feel uncomfortable. It's good to experience some excitement and adrenaline; it makes you feel alive. I know when I'm just a couch potato, I don't feel fear. When I avoid fear, I don't feel alive. When I'm not alive, I'm not growing, I'm not going anywhere in my life. This isn't what you want for your life.

200

Payoffs of Running from Your Fear

There are a few payoffs for avoiding and running from your fear.

Feel free to add to this list:

- You are safe.
- You can stay in bed - all day.
- You can watch TV - all day.
- You don't feel rejection.
- You don't have to confront your future.
- You don't have to do anything.
- You don't have to face your past.
- You don't have to feel afraid.
- You don't have to look at your failures.
- You don't have to take responsibility.
- You don't have to think.
- You don't have to try.
- You don't have to work.
- You get to complain about how things are.
- You get to complain about how things are not.
- You will never fail.

"Being deeply loved by someone gives you strength, while loving someone deeply gives you courage."
~ Lao Tzu

Costs of Running from Your Fear

Here is my list. Make one for yourself, and feel free to use mine and add to it.

- I will be stuck in a relationship, job, and/or home, that I'm not happy with.
- I will feel guilty and shameful about not living my dreams.
- I will not be able to use fear for information.
- I will not be one step closer to having the life I desire.
- I will remain afraid to move forward.
- I won't achieve my goals and mission in life.
- I won't be living the life of my dreams.
- I won't go on my dream vacation.
- I won't have a sense of purposefulness.
- I won't have the benefit of less stress and thus better health.
- I won't have the happiness of knowing I overcame my fear.
- I won't have the joy, happiness, and excitement that I desire.
- I won't have the job I want.
- I won't have the relationship I want.
- I won't see fear as a signal that I'm growing, by moving beyond my comfort zone.

"Don't be afraid of the space between your dreams and reality. If you can dream it, you can make it so."
~Ralph Waldo Emerson

Fear Isn't Natural - It's Learned

When you were born, you only had two fears, a fear of falling and a fear of loud noises. All other fear was learned. A large percentage of your fear came from your parents.

You heard the word 'no' more than any other word. Your parents simply didn't want you to get hurt. You were told to watch out for this and to watch out for that. They told you, don't do this, and don't do that. You were conditioned at a very young age to be afraid.

When I would go on a vacation, my mom would ask, "Are you really going to go?" She would look at the news regarding the country, city, or state where I was going to go and then repeat whatever bad news had occurred there in the last twenty years. She was overly afraid of something happening to me. Our news, movies, and television shows are primarily about crime, car chases, murder, and war. All this media paints a picture of a world that we need to be afraid of.

Some of our religions teach us to be afraid. They tell us to do this, or don't do that. They teach us that if you don't follow the rules, you will be punished and placed in the most horrendous place possible for eternity. They teach us to be afraid, knowing that fear is a motivator to shape our behavior.

We also desperately don't want to look foolish, bad, or to be even the least bit embarrassed. We are so preoccupied in looking good, the thought of looking bad becomes a debilitating fear. When you look at fear for what it really is, you'll begin to realize that fear isn't natural. Fear is developed and learned. Remember, the only natural fears that you were born with are the fears of falling and loud noises. You can reprogram yourself. Know that fear isn't real or natural, that most of your fear you were taught. Know that most fear isn't necessary.

Dream Notes

To Jump-Start Your Dreams

Act as if...
Your dreams have already come true!

Expand Your Comfort Zone and Do Something

In Susan Jeffers' book *Feel the Fear... And Do It Anyway*, Susan uses a grid of nine boxes for each area of your life. She suggests you can work on one area per day, and if you feel better, you can do two or three. You can, for example, aim to improve your relationship with your family. You can call a family member once a week, and that would be growth for you in that area. For me, I might be afraid to call because I might fear being criticized or ridiculed. If I make the call despite my fear, I'll grow, and expand as a result.

Susan encourages you to expand your comfort zone. For me I expand my comfort zone a small amount each time I call my mother, or each time I show up for my appointment to do this writing. When I expand my comfort level, I expand my edge. It gets easier and easier to trust my fear, and to trust that it is helping me. I now trust that my fear is guiding me. My fear is something that I can actually use as a benefit rather than something to stop me from doing things.

Expand your comfort level a little at a time. Think of a time when you did something that you were afraid to do. For example, has there been a time when you spoke in public? If you did, do you remember how good you felt about yourself afterwards? I can expand by doing something as simple as cook a new recipe, or ask a woman for a date. Even if the dish wasn't perfectly prepared or the date didn't happen, I felt better about myself for having tried.

Don't Play the Win Then Game

I will trust my fears after I do something big. I will ask for that raise when I really, really, really deserve it. I'll wait until I lose ten more pounds, then I'll ask for that date. I'll ask for time off after I finish the James project. I'll ask after I have that big win, and my boss will have to say yes. The problem is, I deserve a raise now. The problem is, I could really enjoy a date now. Could my wanting to wait until I finish the James project be a way of avoiding and procrastination? Could it be an excuse?

"I will ask for the date when I get the new car" is an excuse for not confronting my fear of rejection and hearing the word 'no'. I made the word 'no' mean that I'm a defective person. I made the word 'no' mean that I'm a good-for-nothing loser. Can you see how ridiculous this form of thinking is? It's like algebra where the factors X and Y don't always have to go together. I may never lose ten more pounds or get a new car, and I still deserve to have a raise and a date. X doesn't have anything to do with Y. Going on a date has nothing to do with losing ten pounds or having a new car. Asking for a raise has nothing to do with finishing the James project. I'm worthy of a raise whether the James project is finished or not.

Remember in chapter four, your jailor is making excuses for you. So it is really important to be aware when you are playing the win then game, and stop avoiding and start trusting your fears.

In chapter one, you heard about my friend Linda who gets things done. Linda never plays the win then game. When Linda thinks of something that needs to be done, she does it. She doesn't have to worry about winning a game first; it's done.

Not playing the win then game is good for your health. There is much less stress knowing that things are already done. There is less stress not having to win something in order to do or ask for something. It's good for you, and it's good for your dreams.

"All you need is the plan, the road map, and the courage to press on to your destination."
~Earl Nightingale

The Worry Is Worse Than the Doing

Think of a time when you needed to get something done, and fear kept you from doing it. You put it off, and to do it was as simple as making a phone call, balancing your checkbook, or getting your taxes done. The worry and dread is always harder than the doing. After the task is complete, you realized, that wasn't so bad. Asking for the raise, a date, or even getting your taxes done is much easier than the worry. You feel much better having done it. The worry is worse than the doing.

Conclusion

I agree with Dr. Coleman's model of looking at things from the perspective of befriending rather than fighting your fear. It makes perfect sense when you fight something, it will instinctively fight back. Fear is a gift from God. We misuse this gift as an excuse for our jailor to keep us from moving forward. You can trust your fears, go ahead and feel them, accept them, and be aware of them. Fear is something that society, your parents, and you have used to trick yourself from working on your dreams and to keep you safe. Step through and expand your comfort zone, so you can grow and move towards and realize your dreams.

DREAMS
COME
TRUE

Recap — Trust your Fears

Realize That You Are Not Alone: when you realize that you are not the only one, you feel better about your situation.

Don't Take Your Fears So Seriously: most fear isn't real anyway.

Say "Yes" To Your Fear: by accepting your fear, it will lessen.

Realize That Fear Is Your Ally: it is a gift to keep you safe and to give you information.

Payoffs of Running from Your Fear: yes, there are payoffs to having fear.

Coasts of Running from Your Fear: When examined, the costs are too great

Fear isn't Natural, It's learned: know that fear isn't natural, that most of your fear you were taught.

Expand Your Comfort Zone and Do Something: you will feel better about yourself for having tried.

Don't Play the Win Then Game: it is simply a clever form of procrastination.

The Worry Is Worse Than the Doing: most times the worry is harder than the doing.

① Dream Big
② Set goal
③ Take Action

Dreamtime
Do Try This at Home

1. Take your fears for a walk and ask them what they need to do or to learn in order to feel safe concerning the pursuit of your dreams. Quietly walk while you inwardly listen. When the answers come, write them in your journal. Within the next two days, start doing whatever the fear directed you to. Remember, don't worry about being an expert. Just begin.

2. Write at least a half page in your journal about a time when you were fearless. Do that by tomorrow.

3. Buy a fear-reducing candle and burn it while taking an action toward your dreams. (You can use any beautiful candle you name as your fear-reducing candle.)

4. Thank your fears for showing you:
   A. You are on the right track.
   B. What areas you can improve.

5. Consider the consequences for allowing your fears to control you.

Add a few to this list:

- If I allow my fears to control me, I can stay in the same unfulfilling job.
- I'll never be a magnificent husband/wife.
- I'll never take that class.
- I won't finish high school.
- I won't go on a vacation - ever.
- I won't open a McDonald's franchise.

Add a few of your own.

- _____

- _____

- _____

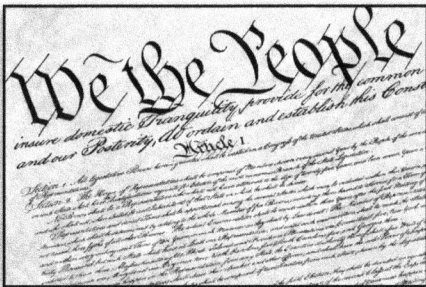

Declaration: I trust my fear. I see fear as a signal that I'm on the right track.

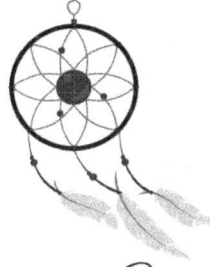

Your
DREAM CATCHER

Chapter X. Treasure Your Family

"My most treasured possessions are not things. They are only things. My friends and family are what counts."

~ Olivia Newton John

Something treasured is something that is highly valued, loved, and of tremendous worth. Family can be a common ancestry or a group of people living together. Family is also your spiritual family. A spiritual family can come from all different communities within your life.

Any group of individuals who come together with common interests can be thought of as family. My softball team is a family. We go out together, eat together, and celebrate with each other. A treasured family is a place to share, shine, unite, and have a safe place where you can work and strive toward your dreams. For example, with my dream to be a magnificent husband, my softball team family is a community where I share, learn, and receive feedback concerning my dream. It is also a safe environment for me to fully express myself.

Why Treasure Your Family

Your family, especially your birth family, shapes your values for you when you are growing up, values that will help you to establish, maintain, and reach your goals and dreams. Your family helps you recognize who you are and what's important to you. What qualities do you want in life? What qualities do you want to instill in yourself to realize and live your dreams, qualities that include integrity, trust, responsibility, honesty, and honor, qualities such as generosity, sharing, forgiveness, and gratitude?

Family can help you instill a sense of connection and community. You connect with yourself and gain a sense of belonging, caring, and unconditional love. With family, you really can't make a mistake. With true family, you can't be wrong. With family behind you, you are more willing and able to strive for and reach your goals and dreams.

With family, you don't have to worry about being embarrassed at how you look or what you do. Without having the need to look good, you can focus on what is necessary for your dreams to manifest. Having a family that you treasure gifts you with guidance, and understanding that no one else can provide. You can say most anything to your family, and they will understand. Your family is loving and supportive and is always there for you. Your family provides a safe place to go and to be. Your family also gives you a physical place in your heart to thrive. Reverend Joann says, "It's a place for your dreams to land." As they land with your family, they are going to land in your heart. As your dreams land in your heart, they will manifest in your life.

Family Comes in Many Forms

You may feel that you don't have a family, or the one you have isn't so hot. You can be orphaned; your family members could have passed away, or you could be estranged from them. Your family is more than your family of your ancestry. As stated above, your family can be a spiritual family. Your spiritual family can come from a church, a synagogue, or a temple. Your spiritual family can be your friends, neighbors, or classmates. They can be friends or more distant relatives such as cousins. Your family can be from your Toastmasters club, softball team, or from your yoga class. They all can give you the tools, support, and guidance that a biological family can give you. Your family can motivate, encourage, and inspire you to grow, develop, and create more than you dreamed possible.

Your family can make you stronger and inspire you to find solutions and to release beliefs, thoughts, and behaviors that no longer serve you. Seeing the benefits of family, if you are not close at this time, you might consider reuniting with your birth family. You can build some bridges and make amends as you are considering the benefits of treasuring your family. Your family can be the support you need to realize your dreams.

Catch your dreams

Treasure

* wealth of any kind or in any form
* something of great worth or value

* a person esteemed as rare or precious

Merriam-Webster

Love

Family is actually where you learned to love. The very moment you were born and placed in your mother's arms, you started to learn about how to love. At the core of your dreams is love, a type of love that is unconditional. Additionally with family, you are never dreaming alone.

Your family helps you to have a sense of integrity and respect for yourself, for others, and your dreams. You learn to be loving to others. You learn a sense of devotion and to be a contribution to the world. Making a contribution to the world is what your dreams are about.

With family you can have any dream you choose to dream. Family is a place of support and encouragement. You don't want to approach just anyone and share your dreams. Many people are jealous or envious of your abilities, gifts, and talents, and may discourage you. It takes a family (birth family or spiritual) to offer true unconditional love and encouragement for you to develop your gifts, talents, and abilities. Family gives you the love and emotional support you need to realize your dreams. Family is that cheerleader and loving, supportive arm that makes the difference.

Build Trust, Safety, and Security

You can learn to trust yourself and your dreams. Your family will give you the security and safety to go for your dreams. Family will give you a place to land if you fall short of expectations. Family knows you better than anyone else. They share your values; they understand you, your highs and lows, your successes, and your failures. Your family will help you raise you up and to see the purpose and meaning in your dreams. They will help you get up and take action and to get up when you have fallen down.

Family Is a Mirror

Your family is a mirror of your life. You can see the potential of what your dreams really can be. Family can help you create your dreams. Family, whether spiritual or biological, will be honest and candid with you. Family will tell you when you make a mistake. They will show you who you really are. Who other than family will be direct and tell you the truth regarding you and your dreams? Family will trigger you and push your buttons. Family will stimulate you to grow. Your family will help you discover what you need to work on. Treasure the gift family provides for your learning, and your growth. My mother triggers me a lot, and those triggers help me see gifts that help me grow. I can now see where I have room to grow, so I can now transform to become a better man.

> "Dreams are today's answers to tomorrow's questions."
> ~Edgar Cayce

Family Knows Best

Your biological or spiritual family supports you when you are off track. They will give you encouragement to keep trying, and they will accept you just the way you are and the way you are not.

Your family will give you honest, clear, and valuable feedback, feedback you can use to clarify your path toward your dreams. You will more easily be able to pinpoint what is moving you toward or away from your dreams. With your family's assistance, you will be able to course-correct and modify what you are doing to best move you on a successful path to the completion of your dreams.

Dream Notes

To Jump-Start Your Dreams

Don't take yourself and life too seriously…

Conclusion

Treasuring your family is not something that you say. It's something that you do. Love them no matter what the appearances, no matter how you perceive their actions, or what is happening. Consider their welfare daily. Think about what you can do to make their lives better. Send them and give them love. Give them a call. Forgive them for anything and everything. Thank them for anything and everything, especially the small things. Your actions will instill a feeling and vibration of treasuring your family.

Treasure their shortcomings. Their shortcomings serve as a mirror for you to know what to work on for yourself. They help you to grow. Buy them a gift, send them a card, shoot them an email, or text, give them a call. Keep them in mind. Treasuring your family will help you manifest your dreams. They give you a safe place in your heart, a place where you can go to recharge and re-energize.

Your family gives you honest feedback. They give you unconditional love. They will be a launching pad for your dreams to formulate, grow, and manifest. Your family gives you a place to share your dreams. A dream not shared is not really a dream. Treasuring your family gives you a place to dream, a place to grow, and a place to love.

DREAMS
COME
TRUE

Recap — Treasure Your Family

Why Treasure Your Family: family is a safe place for your dreams to land.

Family Comes in Many Forms: family is more than your birth family.

Love: family is that cheerleader and loving, supportive arm that makes the difference.

Build Trust, Safety, and Security: family will give you a place to land if you fall short of expectations.

Family Is a Mirror: your family will help you discover what you need to work on.

Family Knows Best: your family will give you honest clear, and valuable feedback.

Dreamtime
Do Try This at Home

1. Within the next five days, call three family members (mother/father/siblings/or closest relatives) and set up an appointment. The phone is good, but it's better to meet in person. Describe to them how important they are to your life and to your dreams.

2. Do something special for someone in your spiritual family, someone from your (church, spiritual center, temple, synagogue, school, sports team or club, or social group). Offer to watch their kids or animals. Take them to lunch or the movies. Call them and let them know you appreciate them. Do whatever comes to mind in order to treasure them.

3. Within the next seven days, set up some time to talk to at least two family members. Make one a brother, sister, or cousin, and the other from your spiritual family, and have them share their life and dreams with you. Note the similarities and differences of their dreams to yours. What did you learn about yourself?

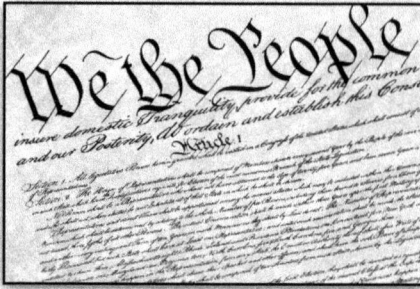

Declaration: My family loves the way I treasure them.

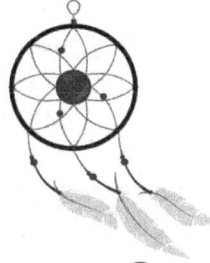

Your
DREAM CATCHER

Chapter XI. Vow to Your Kindest Life

"Too often we underestimate the power of a touch, a smile, a kind word, a listening ear, an honest compliment, or the smallest act of caring, all of which have the potential to turn a life around."

~ Leo F. Buscaglia

Vowing to your kindest life is a promise to perform a certain act, carry out an activity, or behave in a giving way. A vow is a promise or a pledge to someone. A vow is a solemn promise to demonstrate sincerity, inspiration, and reverence. It is a pledge or promise to provide or do something.

Kindness is generosity and warmth. Kindness is showing compassion, courtesy, and caring. Kindness is having and showing a willingness to give time freely. It is showing friendliness to cheer someone up and make them happy. It's in taking the time to listen to, offer a ride to, visit a friend, or better yet, talk to a stranger. My late brother Dan would often help push a stalled car off the road. He once helped a neighbor move in, in the rain. Note: They were someone moving in, therefore they were complete strangers. You can use these qualities to be the best person you can be.

Vowing to your kindest life is congruent to living your dreams. As you give kindness, as you are concerned about people, as you are vowing to commit to kindness, you are making a commitment for your dreams.

The Courage to Be Kind

It takes a tremendous amount of courage to be kind. It can take a lot of courage to do the right thing for the right reasons. Be considerate, compassionate, and kind above everything else. Without the courage to be kind you are not really living your dreams.

My brother Dan was one of the most courageous persons I have known. His courage came from his kindness. He was more interested in helping, assisting, and being there for others than caring and thinking about himself. In college he pushed a girl in a wheelchair to class. Note: This was in 1967, and there were no electric wheelchairs.

On the surface this is a very generous act. What made it courageous was that the woman in the wheelchair was very attractive. Dan's girlfriend was extremely jealous and caused Dan a lot of grief for his act of kindness. Dan had the courage to assist the girl anyway.

This type of behavior, this way of being served Dan later in life. His dream was to be the director of a sheltered workshop for Special Needs individuals. Dan not only became a director, he received numerous awards for doing so. Dan's courage to be kind is what directly led to him fulfilling his dream.

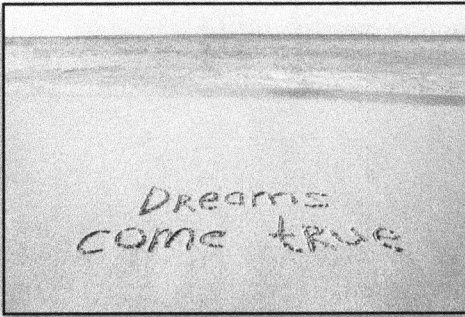

Forgive

* to give up resentment of

* to grant relief from payment of

* to cease to feel resentment against

Merriam-Webster

Vow to Forgive

Forgiving the unforgivable is truly how to vow to your kindest life. What better place to start than the hardest place? Forgive someone you don't want to forgive. Forgiving the so-called unforgivable is a remarkably kind act.

You have had situations where people and/or circumstances in your life have wronged you. Forgiveness is a way to start living your kindest life. It could be a family member, friend, or a business associate. It could be someone who owes you money, cheated you in love, or insulted you and your family. Your life will be that much easier when you release any hate or resentfulness you may have toward them.

The first person you may want to forgive is yourself. Forgiveness is putting aside something or someone who has wronged you. Forgiveness   is loving them anyway. Forgiveness is letting it all go, putting whatever it is aside. Forgiveness is not fostering hate, anger, or resentment, anywhere.

When you truly forgive, you can move forward. You are not tethered to any non-forgiveness, anger, or resentment. Only after forgiving can you move forward. This is why it is important to forgive. You need to forgive to live your dreams and to have the life that you desire and deserve.

Give Service

I love what Reverend Michael Beckwith says, "Live to give." You can start with your family, friends, and neighbors. Make a phone call, give a favor, ask, "What can I do for you?" "Can I walk your dog? Pick up your groceries?" You can just be a friend. Give your time, give your consideration, your thoughtfulness, your kindness. Give service in all areas of your life.

Give, just to give. Don't do it in an effort to gain something. That is inauthentic. Demonstrate kindness just to be kind. Make someone else's life brighter, and your life will be brighter. Give service at your church, spiritual center, synagogue, or mosque. Donate your time, donate your talent, donate your resources. Help out with the Humane Society, a retirement home, the Salvation Army, volunteer at a soup kitchen.

Brainstorm other ways to give service that are interesting to you. Give whatever and wherever you have a passion or interest. Give, and as you are giving, you will be receiving. You will be uplifted, and your dreams will come to you much easier.

Dream Notes

To Jump-Start Your Dreams

Focus on the contribution you can do for others.

Do More Than Is Necessary

You can take that one extra step and do just a little bit more. Jeremy can do a little bit of extra credit. He can come to class early and stay late. He can study a little bit more to help him achieve his dream of a GED. Jeremy could help motivate and inspire his classmates to do better. It's important to do a bit more than is necessary in everything you do. My coach, Rev. Joanne, does much more for me than is agreed, requested, required, necessary, or expected.

By doing more than is necessary, your life works better. You can do more than is expected or necessary with your family, friends, co-workers, and even strangers. By doing more than is necessary, you are vowing to your highest life. Smile and say "hi" to everyone you meet. Give appreciation for especially the small things. When you do more than is necessary, you will see and experience your life expanded and transformed.

Stop It

One behavior a person committed to living their kindest life embodies is to stop complaining. People whom I admire don't complain.They are in a constant state of positivity Complainers are saying things aren't right and repeating it over and over. One method to being your best self is noticing when you complain, and then stop it. The problem is when one is incessant about complaining, they often don't realize what they are doing to themselves. Having being a constant complainer, it seems like a natural way of being. Complainers go so far as to make up things to complain about. They then have something to complain about. For the most part, they do nothing to correct the complaint. Often they aren't even aware of their complaining, and if one isn't aware of their complaining, they can't take action to correct the behavior.

If your dreams are not progressing, one major reason may be that you are too busy complaining to think about your dreams. If you are a constant complainer, you will be complaining about the things that are blocking the accomplishment of your dreams. Ironically the biggest block to achieving your dreams is the complaining. If Jeremy becomes aware of his complaining, he then has the choice to take action to correct the complaint. For example, Jeremy can get a tutor. He can call someone who has already taken the classes for assistance. He can study a little bit more. Jeremy can get some extra instruction or call his study partner. All of these actions are productive and will quiet the complaint. The key is to take committed action.

Another thing we all need to stop is gossiping. Don't talk about other people, and refrain from putting others down. Gossiping has a tendency to circulate back to you and to the target of your gossip. Unless you are that person, no one knows all the circumstances involved. It is impossible and impractical to rightly judge anyone. Jesus stated, "He who is without sin, cast the first stone." We all have issues, and no one is without sin. Stop it. In reality, oftentimes what we are doing is projecting a negative quality about ourselves onto the other person. Stop it. In reality, all you are doing is creating negativity, negativity that will always come straight back to you. A quality to being your best self is not to gossip.

It is also a good plan to stop, really stop to smell the roses. Slow down and enjoy the journey of living and moving toward your dreams. When you stop it and slow down, you can enjoy every moment. Jeremy can stop to realize that it is a wonderful thing he is doing for himself. Stop it and take the time to appreciate yourself. When you stop it and slow down, you can appreciate yourself, what you do, and how you do it.

"Dreams are the touchstones of our character."
~Henry David Thoreau

Another necessary ingredient in achieving your dreams is knowing when and what and when to not stop. Never stop and give up. Winston Churchill said, "Never, never, never, give up." For any dream there will be bumps along the road. See the good in the bumps. With a bump, roadblock, or breakdown comes growth, development, and greater understanding. Stay positive, and when there is a problem, notice it. Realize that there is a benefit, and take a committed action toward a new possibility. You can do more research, call a friend or expert, or change something that you were doing. For example, Jeremy could get a new tutor or take an additional class. I could start asking friends to introduce me to their friends for potential dates. Michelle could consider another franchise to purchase. Your ability to stop it and never give up is a key to living the life of your dreams.

Share Your Dreams

You may not realize how amazing your dreams really are, or you may be shy to share them. You may not believe your dreams are good enough. In truth, it would be considered a sin not to share your gifts, talents, and dreams. Living your dreams and vowing to be kind to yourself means it's imperative to share. Sharing will make your dreams real. When they become real to more and more people, it insures that they become a reality. Do not hold back. People love to hear about others' dreams.

If I gave up on my dream to be a magnificent husband, people wouldn't have the opportunity to see what a great marriage could look like. They wouldn't have the opportunity to be inspired by it. They wouldn't have the chance to take action on their own relationships. Sharing your gifts, talents, and dreams is very important. Sharing is a kind thing to do. Sharing your dreams is about singing your song, writing your book, and dancing your dance.

See the Divine in Everything

Sometimes you forget to appreciate what the Divine has given you. Often circumstances dictate your feelings and thoughts to a point where you forget that the Divine is in everything. If Jeremy can see the good in his teacher when his teacher is having a bad day, then it will be much easier to do his homework, pay attention in class, and to remain excited about his studies. Seeing the good makes working toward your dreams much easier. If I have a date that does not go well, I can focus on what I learned from it. I can then have an idea of what to do better to make the next date more enjoyable. I can remember and see the good in everything, every person, and every situation.

Knowing and seeing the Divine in everything makes life and working towards your dreams wonderful, easy, and natural. You can see that in life you are happier when you realize and recognize there is something larger organizing and orchestrating your life and affairs. You feel better and more positive knowing there is good and wonderful things everywhere.

> "You know you're in love when you can't fall asleep because reality is finally better than your dreams."
> ~Dr. Seuss

Appreciate the Little Things

Say thank you when you normally wouldn't. Appreciate waking up in the morning. Be grateful for your breakfast. Be thankful that you live in a place where you can get a GED, a McDonald's franchise, or a husband or wife. Appreciate that you live in a place where you can actually achieve most anything that you dream of.

There is something special that occurs when you are thankful and appreciative. When you are grateful, thankful, and appreciate it helps make your dreams real. It is saying to yourself and the Universe that you already have it. The subconscious mind doesn't distinguish between something that you deeply think about or what is actual reality. In other words, it doesn't know if your dream actually happened in reality or if it's your imagination. Your gratitude for your dream will automatically activate your subconscious mind to make it happen in reality.

Dream Notes

To Jump-Start Your Dreams

Love Yourself

UNCONDITONALLY

Commit to Understanding

One of the best things you can do to reach your dreams is stop and listen. If I want to be married, listening is important to understanding my potential wife. Jeremy needs to listen to understand his assignments and what is required for his graduation. It is very difficult to have understanding without knowing exactly what is communicated. There is nothing more important than to stop, notice, and listen to understand. It's important for you to commit to understanding to achieve your dreams. Without a blueprint or guide that understanding gives you, you can't fully reach your dreams.

You can also question for clarity. When you aren't 100% sure what has been communicated, ask. Looking good and understanding don't necessary go together. You may think you are too busy to take the time to ask for clarity. Often our lack of clarity and understanding costs a considerable amount of extra time and energy. Take the time to question and to make sure you understand. Take that extra moment to think about what you are up to. Listen and commit to understanding. Understanding is instrumental in achieving and enjoying the achievement of your dreams. It's time to slow down, think, question, and understand.

Guarantee Integrity

It starts with your intention to be sincere, honest, and straightforward in working toward your dreams. Your intention is what you expect and what you want for yourself. Have integrity with your intentions and for your dreams. Have integrity for your goals and plans for every year, month, week, day, hour, and minute. Plan your plan, and work your plan with integrity. Have a solemn vow to be in integrity towards your dreams and towards yourself. Integrity means to honor your word, to be whole and complete with what you say, and do what you said you will do, and when you will do it. When you say or plan to do something, do it.

By having the intention to guarantee integrity, you are honoring yourself and your dreams. You are honoring your word, and for this alone you are living your dreams. You're guaranteeing that you will do and say what you said you would say and do. You are now escaping from your jailor. You are eliminating the bonds that had held you back. You are getting things done. You are progressing toward your dreams and living completely honestly and in integrity with yourself and your dreams.

Your integrity will keep you on track, on your path, and consistent with your purpose for your dreams. Saying what you will do and doing what you said you will do are two large and wonderful steps toward living your dreams. If you are not in integrity with your dreams, if you don't vow and guarantee integrity, you won't achieve your desires. You won't enjoy the process or the journey. You also won't enjoy the results. When you vow and guarantee to live your dreams, you are living a life that matters.

Conclusion

As you vow to be your best self in complete integrity, magic occurs. When you do what you say you are going to do, when you do what is expected of you, even if not asked, your life transforms. You are demonstrating to yourself and your dreams that you and your dreams matter. You are declaring you are out to make an impact on the world. You are announcing that, "I'm out to make a contribution to the life of others." You start by not taking details lightly. See to it that you set priorities and you stick to them. Do the most important tasks first thing in the morning. Vow to be your best self, to live your kindest life. And then do it. Make being the kindest person you can be a way of living.

Recap — Vow to Your Kindest Life

The Courage to Be Kind: being kind is key to living the life of your dreams.

Vow to Forgive: when you truly forgive, you can move forward.

Give Service: you will be uplifted, and your dreams will come to you much easier.

Do More Than Is Necessary: when you do more than is necessary, you will see and experience your life expanded and transformed.

Stop It: people who are living their dreams stay positive and don't complain.

Share Your Dreams: sharing makes your dreams become more real.

See the Divine in Everything: you feel better and more positive knowing there is good and wonderful things everywhere.

Appreciate the Little Things: when you are grateful, thankful, and appreciative, it helps make your dreams real.

Commit to Understanding: understanding is instrumental in achieving and enjoying the achievement of your dreams.

Guarantee Integrity: when you vow and guarantee to live your dreams, you are living a life that matters.

Dreamtime
Do Try This at Home

1. For no reason, do something kind. Take your neighbor's trash out. Wash their car. Help a lady across the street. Pay the tab for the person behind you at Starbucks. Buy a newspaper and give it to a complete stranger. Make up something on your own. If it feels good, do it again. If it doesn't feel good, try something else until it does. Write about it in your journal.

2. For the next week whenever you get the chance: Give way to other drivers. Yes, allow them to go in front of you.
   a. Notice if you have any resistance.
   b. After a few days, see if there is any change in your resistance.
   c. Be aware of any differences in your driving or your perspective toward other drivers and yourself.
   d. Are you more caring (kind) toward them? Are you calmer and in less of a hurry? If so, is this helpful to you in achieving your dreams?

3. Be of service, volunteer, assist, and do something kind. You can be of assistance for your church, school, kids'

school, the city, the local shelter or animal rescue. Start within the next two weeks and keep it up. Pay attention to your life. How does this activity help you and your dreams? Document your insights in your journal.

4. Next time you go out to lunch with your friends or co-workers, do the unexpected. Pick up the check, leave an outrageously large tip, or buy a round of beverages. Say it's just something you want to do, just to be kind. How did you feel afterwards? Could it help you be more receptive to your good and to your dreams?

Declaration: I choose to live my kindest life. Today I will be kind-because that is who I am and what I do!

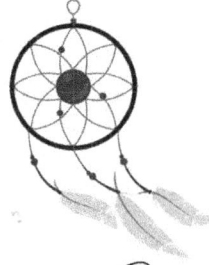

Your DREAM CATCHER

Chapter XII. Vow to Be True to Your Dreams

"I seal this prayer in faith, trust, and truth, Amen."

~ Jesus

Congratulations, you made it to the last chapter. This book has given you a format, guideline, and a template to catch your dreams and to live the life you have dreamed about. The exercises have put you in a position to believe, and to trust in yourself, your dreams, and the process. You have become your own *Dream Catcher*.

Vow to your dreams as you would in marriage. Choose to make a strong commitment to a life you love. Sharing your dreams and your vows with others will help them become real. Everyone whom you enroll in your dreams, by their enrollment will help manifest your dreams. As more and more of your friends and relatives see your dreams as a possibility, your dreams become more of a probability. When you make a vow to your dreams, you are committing to your highest and best life, your highest and best you.

A vow is a solemn promise to perform a certain act, to carry out an activity, or a behavior as sacred. A vow is a promise or pledge to someone or something. It is a promise to assure that something will be done. A solemn promise to your dreams demonstrates sincerity, authenticity, and commitment. Your vow is observed as sacred and engenders reverence. Your dreams are worthy of reverence, sincerity, commitment, and more!

The first thing to do in making a vow may sound counter-intuitive. The place to start in making a vow to your dreams is from nothing. Coming from a place of nothing creates a space for unlimited possibilities to occur. Your dreams and vows to your dreams are better served if they come from a place and space of unlimited possibilities. Unlimited possibilities means there are no restrictions or limitations. This way your dreams have the ability to expand and to be created and re-created to be even more than you may have originally dreamed. Can it get any better?

To have a true vow, you need to get a divorce from how you thought your dreams should be. You need to remove everything, including any preconceived ideas of how they should look. It is best when you are an opening or clearing for your dreams to grow and breathe.

A vow is a genuine, loyal, and faithful commitment to be a cause in the matter of the realization of your dreams. Divorce yourself from anything but the attainment of your dreams. Your dreams need room, or a space in which to take place. It is known in physics that nature will fill up an empty space. Aristotle taught that, "Nature abhors a vacuum." Creating a divorce on how your dreams should look and how they are to be brought about creates room, or a space for your dreams to develop, grow, and manifest.

"Do not lose hold of your dreams or aspirations. For if you do, you may still exist but you have ceased to live."
~Henry David Thoreau

Empty the Dungeon

It is time to get rid of the blockages that are preventing you from moving toward your dreams. Let your negative thinking, your thoughts of being less than, your feelings of not being good enough out of your self-made dungeon. Know that anything is possible and that your dreams are achievable. Go out and try. That way you won't have any regrets.

Use your journal as a place for clarity regarding your dreams and your self-made dungeon. Knowing and putting your thoughts, activities, and dreams on paper helps you to empty your dungeon. When you journal, you will gain insight to what is blocking you. Ironically, your biggest block is yourself. Your awareness is enough to exterminate your dragons and remove them from your dungeon.

When you experience the clarity that writing or journaling gifts you, you are free to pursue your dreams. For instance, the writing of this book, I have all of the chapters' titles and topics for each chapter posted on the wall in front of me in my bedroom. I can clearly see what I need to do. I can't deny that there is a book in front of me, ready to be written. All I have to do is fill in the blanks around the chapters and topics within each chapter. It is already there. The contents of your journal can give you the same clarity and guidelines for your dreams.

Journaling also heals the emotional aspects of your not getting started. Seeing the steps in front of me gets me going. I know exactly what to do to complete this book. It can be the same for you once you have the steps in front of you. Your steps don't have to be perfect and are subject to change. The point is you can actually see and know that the steps to achieving your dream are real. With a written format, you can remove any blame, shame, or guilt. You can illuminate and then eliminate the blocks. You can empty the dungeon and say yes to your dreams.

Catch your dreams

Faithfull

* steadfast in affection or allegiance

* firm in adherence to promises or in observance of duty

* given with strong assurance

Merriam-Webster

From Vendetta to a Vow of Faithfulness

A vendetta is like the famous feud between the Hatfields and the McCoys. The irony of their disagreement was that they forgot why they were mad at each other. Nevertheless, they didn't give up on fighting, arguing, and being hostile toward each other. This kind of vendetta will prevent you from moving toward your dreams.

An example of a vendetta is the shameful way many punish our parents for whatever we thought that they did or didn't do perfectly for us. We often go on a vendetta or feud and consciously or unconsciously decide to be unsuccessful as a method to punish them. We believe we punish them by not living our dreams. Regrettably this sounds ridiculous, and sadly, is extremely common.

> "A dream you dream alone is only a dream. A dream you dream together is reality."
> ~Yoko Ono

To move from vendetta to a vow of faithfulness, you begin by making a promise to be faithful. You begin by firmly believing in yourself and your dreams. You can move from vendetta to a vow of faithfulness by removing the blocks that prevent you from your vow of faithfulness.

Realize that many people will be positively impacted by you working toward your dreams. You will affect people by inspiring them to move toward their own dreams. You could inspire someone such as Jeremy to get his GED. You will influence someone like me to not give up on their book. It is so important for one to achieving their dreams to see someone else who is not willing to give up on their dreams.

I can show my parents how much they hurt me by giving up on my dreams. My vendetta to hurt myself and thus somehow hurt them by not being successful is like trying to hurt someone else, when I'm the one who drank the poison. When you choose to not drink the poison, to let the vendetta go, and move to a vow of faithfulness, you are well on your way to achieving and living your dreams.

Your Word is Your Bond

A bond is the way things stick together. It's a link that bonds people together in relationships. Webster defines bond as, "a solemn agreement." A bond is a promise to do something.

It is perfectly fine to bond to your dreams by talking to them. Go ahead and talk to your dreams. They will listen, and they will respond. Like a plant, your dreams will respond to your speaking to them in a positive and loving manner. Expressing your love for your dreams will help them grow. Your speaking positive toward them gives them energy and life.

Dream Notes

To Jump-Start Your Dreams

Affirm-Out Loud 100x's a Day

"My Dreams are Real."

The Beauty of Loyalty

Loyalty looks, feels, and sounds right, and it's beautiful. Loyalty to your dreams gives them purpose and meaning. When you see beauty, you are attracted to it and can't take your eyes off of it. When your dreams are seen as beautiful, loyalty is naturally created. The beauty of loyalty helps you to manifest your dreams. It is easy for your dreams to become a reality because your dreams are beautiful.

Hug Your Dreams

Embrace your dreams. When you embrace something, you take it in. You totally and unconditionally accept it. You are protecting and nurturing your dreams. You are staying on track and focused towards the realization of your dreams.

Embrace your vow to totally say yes to your dreams. Say, "I'm going to do all that it takes to manifest my dreams." Do everything and whatever it takes. Hug and hang on to your dreams. Announce your vows, hug your dreams, and go for your dreams-no matter what.

Seal Your Vow with a Kiss

What is the first thing a couple does when they are pronounced husband and wife? That's right, they seal their vow with a kiss. A seal closes something tightly and securely with the purpose to prevent tampering. A kiss will seal your vow, meaning it is sealed and secure by your promise to be true to your dreams.

A kiss is a very soft, subtle touch. A kiss is a way of saying, "Yes," a way of sealing your vow. A kiss has moisture; moisture creates the seal. A kiss symbolizes a feeling of love for your dreams. With your dreams, like a marriage, you are sealing it. You are being true to it. You are protecting it from harm. A kiss makes it sweet; it makes it tender. Your dreams are worthy of being loved, of being protected, of being nurtured. Your sealing your vow to your dreams with a kiss gives importance to it.

Conclusion

There is something almost magical that occurs when you make a vow, a commitment to something. When you commit a vow to your dreams, you create momentum for its realization. You are saying to yourself and the Universe that you are serious, that you plan to make your dreams real, that you are ready to catch your dreams and live them.

DREAMS
COME
TRUE

Recap — Vow to Be True to Your Dreams

Empty the Dungeon: get rid of the blockages that are preventing you from moving toward your dreams.

From Vendetta to a Vow of Faithfulness: let go of resentments and be true to yourself, your family, and your dreams.

Your Word is Your Bond: bond to your dreams by talking to them.

The Beauty of Loyalty: the beauty of loyalty helps you to manifest your dreams.

Hug Your Dreams: embrace and say "Yes" to your dreams.

Seal Your Vow with a Kiss: Your dreams are worthy of being loved, protected, and nurtured.

Dreamtime
Do Try This at Home

1. Write a vow to each of your top three dreams. Use a beautiful font and paper. Display it where you can see and read it out loud every day for twenty-one days (see appendix #5).

2. Dedicate a piece of jewelry (a ring, necklace, tie pen, watch, bracelet) as a symbol of your vow to your dreams. Wear it continuously for at least a month. Continually keep in mind the reason you are wearing it.

3. Make a promise to yourself that you will continue to strive for your dreams, **no matter what**. Write about your determination and commitment in your journal.

4. Celebrate your vows with friends and family. (Go out to dinner, coffee, dancing, etc.) Let them know why you are having the celebration.

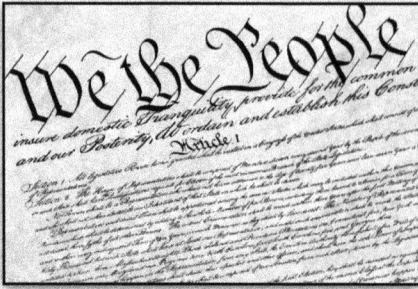

Declaration: I vow to manifest and make my dreams real.

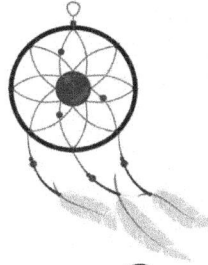

Your
DREAM CATCHER

Conclusion

"Dreams become reality when we put our minds to it."

~Queen Latifah

You have goals and aspirations you want to accomplish in life. We call them dreams. Your dreams are the most important things that you desire in life. If you could be, do, or have anything you wanted, it would be for your dreams to be fulfilled.

You began by daring to dream your dreams. Then you created and charted a plan. Your chart is your roadmap on how you are going to progress toward your dreams. Then you came to the realization that it is best to have a guide or coach to usher you to the realization of your dreams. It is not enough to just have a coach; you need to learn to be in a position to be coachable, to be guidable. You learned about the aspects that tend to sabotage you on your path. The saboteurs, rascals, or hecklers that tend to block, and discourage you to get you off track. You discovered how to love yourself, and particularly, how it is important to love your body. With a healthy body you can be in a position to enjoy your dreams and to enjoy your journey.

You learned how to succeed. You learned the steps to remarkable success. You recognized the importance to tending to your dreams daily and to follow your intuition. You now can recognize the importance of a daily practice to help you move towards living the life of your dreams. The next step after following your intuition is allowing God, Spirit, or your higher self to be present in your life so you can have more insights available to help you manifest your dreams. Next, you discovered to trust your fears. You learned that fears can be an ally, friend, or guide.

You read about the importance or treasuring your family, biological and spiritual. Then you discovered the importance of kindness. Living your kindest life projects love and cooperation, which are returned to you. Being kind brings meaning to your dreams. Finally, you took a vow to be true to your dreams. You discovered in taking vows, you are committing a solemn promise to strive, work, and to live your dreams. You are making a commitment to live your kindest life, to treasure your family, to trust your fears, to follow your intuition, to tend to your dreams, and your life daily. This book has been a journey from daring to vow, to risking, and trusting, to the manifesting of your most cherished dreams. As you play with the Dreamtime exercises at the end of each chapter, you live the life you desire, the life you love, the life of your dreams. You become, Your Dream Catcher.

David KLINE LOVETT

Appendix #1

The Heckler's Prime Directives

1. The Heckler's prime directive is to not be expose
2. To prevent you from any possible risk.
3. To prevent you from any possible failure.
4. To prevent you from feeling.
5. To intensify.
6. To create a feeling of overwhelm.
7. To create as much confusion as possible.
8. Get you to STOP-no matter what.
9. To make you work harder.
10. To make you sick.
11. To make you tired.
12. To prevent you from thinking.
13. To keep you busy, preoccupied, unorganized, depressed, frustrated, forgetful, and numb.
14. To save you from pain.
15. To keep you from anything new, different, or exciting.
16. To keep you away from relationships.
17. To stop you from taking action.
18. To get you to be perpetually mad and frustrated with yourself.
19. To get you to forget your dreams.
20. To believe your dreams are impossible, impractical, unrealistic, and better for someone else.
21. To complicate.
22. To get you to blame everyone and everything for your problems.
23. To keep you in a state of denial regarding your life, yourself, and your goals and dreams.

Appendix #2

Here are a few of the times when it's your inner Heckler doing the talking:

- Anytime you procrastinate on your life and dreams.

- At the times you feel unorganized, frustrated, disoriented, lost, overwhelmed, sick, tired, shameful, embarrassed, not worthy, guilty, or confused.

- When for no reason you just don't feel like it.

- When you are easily distracted or do something completely different.

- When you intensify the work you are doing, making it more complicated and difficult.

- When you plan to work on a project and choose to do something else.

- When you rationalize why you are not moving toward your goals and dreams.

- Whenever you refuse to put goals and dreams on paper.

- When you talk yourself out of working toward your dreams. For example, rather than moving toward your dreams, you talk yourself into watching television, going to the movies, checking emails, playing with Facebook, or calling a friend. You reason with yourself that you will do it later.

Appendix #3

<u>21 Skills for outwitting your inner Heckler</u>

1. Follow your calling.
2. Be guided by your yearning.
3. Get close to all people.
4. Notice your place in the world.
5. Do some things.
6. Serve somebody.
7. Contribute to somebody's life.
8. Create safety for somebody's life.
9. Laugh at the ridicules (the Heckler).
10. Forgive others and yourself.
11. Master your self-talk.
12. Finish your grieving.
13. Share your healing story.
14. Be an audience to another's victory.
15. Refuse to leave it to Beaver.
16. Risk everything for love.
17. Heal your inner pessimist.
18. Blame no one.
19. Forgive your not knowing.
20. Repeat: "It was like this-**Until Today.**"
21. Love your inner Heckler.

Appendix #4

The Heckler's Rants

The Heckler's rants are in the first person (Stealth).
We think the rants are our own.

Amnesia	I forget, what are my dreams again?
Blame	It's your fault.
Confusion	I don't know what to do and/or in what order, better do nothing.
Desperation	I have to do it. If I don't get it done, everyone will know that I'm a loser.
Embarrassment	I'm too embarrassed, I might appear foolish, I better not even try. That way no one will know I'm no good.
Frustration	It's just too hard, I'm too old, I can't figure it out, I don't know where to start, I got to get away from this work.
Guilt	I feel guilty for not working on my dreams. I'll just quit.
Hopelessness	My dreams seem hopeless. I don't want to even try.
Intensifies	I need to do everything. Now.
Lack of Focus	I'll do this instead, or maybe this, and this looks interesting.

Modifies
I think the process needs to be changed, and then I'll change it again.

Not Good Enough/Low Self-Esteem I'll never do it, I can't do it.

Over-Analyzing There must be a better way to do this.
Negative Self-Talk I can't do it, I won't do it right, everyone will laugh.

Overwhelm/Too Busy There is too much to do. I give up, I'll do it when I feel more like it.

Perfectionistic I have to do it perfect the first time, otherwise I can't do it.

Procrastination I'll do it later, some other time. Right now it's time to play.

Reprimand I'm a no-good loser. I never finish what I start.

Self-Critical I'm not good. I'm not smart enough, I'm a real work.

Shame I won't look good, and people will make fun of me. Everyone will know I'm stupid. I should have done it sooner.

To Sick and/or Tired I'm sick and tired, I'll do it later, I'll rest or better yet, watch TV and then I'll do it when I feel better.

Unorganized/Clutter It's just too hard to focus, I can't find anything.

Appendix #5

<u>Tools to Transform the Heckler into Your Hero</u>

1. ACT: Don't get bogged down with too many options.

2. Fight for your life.

3. Focus on one thing at a time.

4. Forget perfectionism: Let go of the notion that anything less than perfect is unacceptable. Write it down:

5. Get help.

6. Grow thicker skin.

7. Learn about the Heckler.

8. Listen for signs of the Heckler.

9. Plan your dreams and actions.

10. Risk: Be willing to fail, to look foolish, to try something new.

11. Think: Take time and think about what they are doing to take your life away.

12. Who, what, where, why, and how you are going to transform the Heckler.

Appendix #6

<u>Vow to My Dream</u>

I _____, promise you _____
      (Name)   (Dream)

to honor, respect, and to never give up on thee. I vow to be

faithful and forsake distractions, perfectionism, intensifying,

modifying, feelings of overwhelm, and procrastination toward

you _____, I will be true to you in good times
       (Dream)

and especially in bad, in health and in sickness. I will

continue to strive and do everything in my power to move

with you, and to be closer to you every day of my life.

_____   _____
        Name   Date

Appendix #7

If's, that are blocking you from catching your dreams

If I didn't have a wife and family …
If I had enough "pull" …
If I had money …
If I had a good education ….
If I could get a job …
If I had good health …
If I only had time …
If times were better …
If other people understood me …
If conditions around me were only different …
If I could live my life over again …
If I did not fear what "they" would say …
If I had been given a chance …
If I now had a chance …
If other people didn't "have it in for me" …
If nothing happens to stop me …
If I were only younger …
If I could only do what I want …
If I had been born rich …
If I could meet "the right people" …
If I had the talent that some people have …
If I dared assert myself …
If I only had embraced past opportunities …
If I only had somebody to help me.
If my family understood me …
If I lived in a big or small city …
If I could just get started …
If I were only free …
If I had the personality of some people …

If I were not so fat or thin …
If my talents were known …
If I could just get a break …
If I could only get out of debt …
If I hadn't failed …
If I only knew how …
If everybody didn't oppose me …
If I didn't have so many worries …
If I could marry the right person ..
If people weren't so dumb …
If my family were not so extravagant …
If I were sure of myself …
If luck were not against me …
If I had not been born under the wrong star …
If it were not true that "what is to be will be" …
If I did not have to work so hard …
If I hadn't lost my money …
If I lived in a different neighborhood …
If I didn't have a "past" …
If I only had a business of my own.
If other people would only listen to me …

**** IF I HAD THE COURAGE TO SEE MYSELF AS I REALLY AM …

Appendix #8

<u>Behaviors to Be a Husband</u>

1. Always see the Divine in her-no matter what!

2. Constantly consider methods to improve her life.

3. Constantly listen unconditionally and speak honestly.

4. Continually give, share, and think of her.

5. Create and maintain a sparkling home and car.

6. Heal my past with my family and myself.

7. Keep myself impeccably groomed.

8. Love, honor, and respect all women.

9. Maintain a healthy mind, body, and spirit.

10. Study and learn communication and relationship skills.

11. To love myself unconditionally.

x

---

x

Appendix #9

<u>My Dreams</u>

1. To Be a Magnificent Husband

2. To Complete this Book

3. To Restore Myself to Health

Appendix #10

10 Things to Do to Save Me

1. Ask God for Help...Pray

2. Call a Prayer Hotline.

3. I have friends -- Call One...
   a. Betty Jones cell 555-555-5555
   b. Brent Homes 555-555-5555
   c. Debbie Barney 555-555-5555
   d. John Smith 555-555-5555
   e. Kathy Gates 555-555-5555
   f. Mary Goodman 555-555-5555

4. Run toward my eight-year-old self, and get him/her an ice cream

5. My Mom, Dad, Sister, and Brother Love me... Call Them...

6. Scream into the Scream Pillow

7. Stop everything....Go love your pet

8. Stop the Heckler

9. Take yourself to the Beach, or Park-NOW!!!!!!

10. Welcome my sadness and Grief

Appendix #11

My Vision Wish List

1. Be a model boyfriend/husband
2. Be a Distinguished Toastmaster
3. Be a great lover
4. Be completely well
5. Do stand-up comedy, once a month or more
6. Feel great and have massive energy
7. Finish this book
8. Forgive everyone
9. Forgive myself
10. Have a love affair with myself
11. Have a fit body
12. Have abundant energy all day long
13. Make big money public speaking
14. Produce three flute (CDs)
15. Produce weight-loss, real estate, network marketing, sales, find a job, confident speaker, find a girlfriend, and get god grades meditation (CD)
16. To be in love
17. To be an example of someone who is healthy
18. To help people heal
19. Visit Africa
20. Visit Alaska
21. Visit Amsterdam
22. Visit Canada
23. Visit Egypt
24. Visit India
25. Visit New Zealand
26. Visit Paris
27. Visit Peru
28. Write books on Comedy, Real Estate, Public Speaking, and Full Self Expression

Appendix #12

Major Points to be a Great Coachee

1. Ask questions when you don't understand.

2. Be appreciative and remember all your coach has done.

3. Be available & ready to do everything your coach says.

4. Be prepared and ready early for each meeting.

5. Communicate by asking questions.

6. Comprehend the brilliance of your coach.

7. Consider all of the classes, workshops, books your coach has read, all the monies spent for his/her education.

8. Consider their talents and all the hats your coach has to wear to help and assist you.

9. Make sure you know exactly what it is that was intended for you to be.

10. Pay attention and get your reactive mind out of the way.

11. Remember, your coach is working for you and your dreams.

12. Stay excited, enthusiastic, motivated, and in love with your dreams.

13. Stay on track and in integrity.

Appendix #13

<u>Dream Board</u>

Recommended Readings and References

1. *A Course in Miracles*, Foundation for Inner Peace, Viking, 1975
2. Barker, Raymond Charles. The Power of Decision, Dodd Mead & Company, 1968
3. Beckwith, Michael Bernard. Lifevisioning, Sounds True, 2012.
4. Beckwith, Michael Bernard. Spiritual Liberation, Atria Books, 2008.
5. Blanchard, Ken & Shula, Don. Everyone's a Coach, Zondervan Publishing House, 1995.
6. Canfield, Jack. Hansen, Mark Victor. Hewitt, Les. The Power of Focus, Health Communications, 2000.
7. Campbell, Joseph. The Hero's Journey, New World Library
8. Carnegie, Dale. How to Win Friends & Influence People, Pocket Books, 1936.
9. Carson, Rick. Taming Your Gremlins. Quill, 2003.
10. Choquette, Sonia. Your Heart's Desire, *Three Rivers* PRESS, 1997.
11. Covey, Stephen R. The 7 Habits of Highly Effective People, Simon & Schuster, 1989
12. Dyer, Wayne. Manifest Your Destiny, Harper Collins Publishers 1997.
13. Dyer, Wayne. Excuses Begone!, Hay House, 2009.
14. Dyer, Wayne. Power Of Intention, Hay House, 2004.
15. Fournies, Ferndiand. Coaching for improved work performance, McGraw-Hill, 2000.
16. Gee, Judee. Intuition: Awakening Your Inner Guide, Barnes & Noble, 1999.
17. Hill, Napoleon. Think and Grow Rich, Fawcett Books, 1937.
18. Jeffers, Susan. Feel the Fear and Do It Anyway, Fawcett Books, 1987.
19. Karges, Craig. Ignite Your Intuition, Health Communications, Inc.1999.

20. Levine, Terri. Stop Managing Start Coaching, CCU Press, 2003.

21. Maxwell, John C. My Dream Map, Thomas Nelson, 2009.
21. McKay, Matthew. Fanning, Patrick, Self Esteem, Barnes & Noble, 2000.
23. Rosanoff, Nancy. Intuition Workout, Aslan Publishing, 1988.
24. Shine, Florence Shovel. The Game of Life and how to play it, DeVorss Publications, 1925.
25. Sinter, Marsha, Do What You Love The Money Will Follow, Dell Publishing, 1987.
26. Thibodeau, Lauren. Natural-Born Intuition, New Page Books The Career Press, 2005.
27. Tracy, Brian. Flight Plan, The Real Secret of Success, Berrett-Koehler Publisher, Inc. 2008.
28. Vaughan, Frances E. Awakening Intuition, Anchor Books, 1979.
29. Whitmore, John. *Coaching for Performance*. Nicholas Brealey Publishing, 1992.
30. Wooden, John. They Call Me Coach, McGraw-Hill Companies Inc. 1988.

About the Author

David Kline Lovett began his spiritual journey in 1996 as a result of a painful divorce. He was motivated to make something positive come as a result of the separation. In 1997 David began studying many forms of spirituality. David researched Shamanism, Buddhism, the law of attraction, and many teachings and authors such as Neal Donald Walsch, Earnest Holmes, A Course in Miracles, Lee Carroll-Kryon, Abraham-Hicks, and Osho.

In 1999, David found Religious Science, a teaching that synthesized the wisdom of the ages. In 2002 David completed a three-year program to become a Religious Science Certified Practitioner (RScP). In 2016 David transferred his Practitioner license to the Agape International Spiritual Center, and became an Agape Licensed Spiritual Practitioner (ALSP) to deepen his spiritual journey. He has remained in class as a student, assistant, or facilitator until the present.

From 2006 through 2012 David thrived under the tutelage of Dr. Reverend Joanne Colman, who coached him in the skills of writing, spirituality, and humanitarianism.

Mr. Lovett is a skilled public speaker and holds the highest designation from Toastmasters International, the (DTM) Distinguished Toastmaster Award. In June of 2013 David began taking courses and seminars from the world leading professional and personal development company-Landmark. In March of 2016 David completed the highly recognized and transformational Introduction Leaders Program and became an Introduction Leader for Landmark.

Mr. Kline Lovett is a Native American flute artist, and is a regular musician for meditations at The Agape International Spiritual Center and Spectra Yoga Studio. David is also a avid comedian, and even worse a book on comedy-*Comedy Made Easy*. David is primarily invested, interested, and excited to be assisting others to realize their goals, dreams, and full self-expression. You can view his other products at the beginning of this book, or go to davidklinelovett.com.

www.ingramcontent.com/pod-product-compliance
Lightning Source LLC
Chambersburg PA
CBHW060257100426
42742CB00011B/1789